Resistance Heroines in Nazi- and Russian-occupied Austria

Resistance Heroines in Nazi- and Russian-occupied Austria

Anschluss and After

Tim Heath, Virginia Wells and Herti Bryan

PEN & SWORD
HISTORY

First published in Great Britain in 2021 by
Pen & Sword History
An imprint of
Pen & Sword Books Ltd
Yorkshire – Philadelphia

ISBN 978 1 52678 787 3

Typeset by Mac Style
Printed and bound in the UK by
CPI Group (UK) Ltd, Croydon CR0 4YY

Pen & Sword Books Limited incorporates the imprints of Atlas,
Archaeology, Aviation, Discovery, Family History, Fiction, History,
Maritime, Military, Military Classics, Politics, Select, Transport,
True Crime, Air World, Frontline Publishing, Leo Cooper, Remember
When, Seaforth Publishing, The Praetorian Press, Wharncliffe
Local History, Wharncliffe Transport, Wharncliffe True Crime
and White Owl.

For a complete list of Pen & Sword titles please contact

PEN & SWORD BOOKS LIMITED
47 Church Street, Barnsley, South Yorkshire, S70 2AS, England
E-mail: enquiries@pen-and-sword.co.uk
Website: www.pen-and-sword.co.uk

Or

PEN AND SWORD BOOKS
1950 Lawrence Rd, Havertown, PA 19083, USA
E-mail: Uspen-and-sword@casematepublishers.com
Website: www.penandswordbooks.com

Contents

Introduction

The door is opened by a sprightly, silver-haired lady and at once I am greeted with a barrage of questions: 'Hello, hello! Where's the dog? Ah, there he is! How *are* you? Have you brought Raya? Come in, come in! Would you like tea?' We settle comfortably into her big armchairs and I notice the beautifully ironed arm covers and the embroidered cloth on the coffee table. Everything in this room is neat and precise, echoing the personality of my friend and neighbour, Herta, who always prefers to be called Herti.

Chief, the black Lab, has a good snuffle around and Herti jumps up to fetch him a bowl of water and a 'treat'. Satisfied and knowing this is a good place to be he, too, settles down at our feet, aware we could be here for some time. My notebook is handy, and we embark on another episode of Herti's fascinating life story – I ask the questions now and she revisits her childhood and early schooldays. Her face is radiant and full of love as she tells me about her family and the wonderful time before her life was shaken to the core by war.

Herti is 90 now – she celebrated her big birthday last February. I didn't really know her until later in the spring: for sure I knew who she was – we live in a small village with a strong community 'vibe' so most people know who lives where. Herti and I live a mere 200 yards from each other yet had not really met other than to say 'hello'. What changed this was that, through my connection with our Mullion Carers Group, we set up an IT course in the village aimed at supporting older residents to become more confident using their computers. Word spread fast and soon we had more than 30 members coming along to our sessions, delivered by CRCC (Cornwall Rural Community

Charity) and funded by, initially, Nat West and subsequently by Aged Veterans. Herti heard about the course and came along, bringing her lively personality and enthusiasm to learn something new with her. At the start we were all asked what we hoped to get from the course and what particular skills we wanted to learn. Immediately Herti announced that she wanted help to get her book completed – she had come so far with research and initial drafting, thanks to the efforts and support of a couple of other friends, but had reached a bit of an impasse. I had heard that Herti had had an interesting life and said I would be happy to help develop her project – perhaps she would let me read through what she had, and I could have a think about how to proceed.

So, we came together through this project and I quickly realized that this lady's story needed to be completed. I had so many questions and, as we worked through each stage, so the story began to take on its 'shape', developing chronologically and becoming an account of many remarkable events.

As we worked through each 'chapter' of Herti's life, she was continually surprised and amazed by the events: 'I can't believe I did that!' or 'How did I get away with that?' constantly punctuated our conversations. Herti had harboured the idea for most of her life, as so many older war survivors do, that the horrors of the past had to be confined to history and not revisited: after the war it was important to focus on the present and the future and the business of 'getting on with life' prevented retrospection. Herti had not discussed her experiences with others, even her mother – though they had had countless opportunities to do so during their many visits and holidays together over the years. Now it was too late to ask questions of others. But the time had come to face the past and record her memories before they, too, were beyond recall.

Describing her earliest memories, a picture emerged of a lively, inquisitive child, adored by her parents and who enjoyed the doting love and attention of a wide, extended family. Herti's adventurous spirit was apparent early on – how she enjoyed the excursions with her family, and she was always prepared to 'have a go' at any new experience. She was athletic and sporty and has remained active throughout her life. Even now, though troubled by painful knees and some of the other annoying side effects of advancing years, she finds ways to 'keep going', she exercises as much as possible and keeps fit and healthy. She is still inquisitive, keeping up to date with current affairs and forming sensible, reasoned opinions on a variety of topics. She is fascinated by medical and scientific developments and the amazing abilities of the human race to be compassionate, caring and altruistic yet also to be the perpetrators of horrors beyond comprehension. One of her repeated exclamations is that the world is peopled by billions who all share the same essential physical attributes yet who are all diverse and unique.

Every time we meet – and we get together every week for a planning session – we chatter away about books and films and what's going on in the village and the world ... before eventually getting down to the task. More than once I have felt it a great shame that Herti was deprived of the chance of a university education and of fulfilling her ambition to become a doctor. She would have brought common sense, warmth and intelligence to that vocation. However, I am constantly aware that Herti is someone who has made the most of the limitations imposed upon her and has always found a way through difficulties. She studied hard and loved learning, especially the English language, which proved absolutely essential in her role as translator. It would have been socially unacceptable for her, as a married woman and Austrian living in the UK, to embark on a career in medicine in the post-war period. In any case, by then Herti was focused on her promise to her father to look after her mother and sister. This sense of commitment has remained with her throughout her life and, she tells me, was a significant factor in her decision not to have a family of her own. Her sister Mädy still lives in Graz and Herti speaks with her frequently thanks to the wonders of Skype. Nowadays the prospect of getting together is more problematic – despite the ten-year age difference travel presents challenges for both of them. Herti has a niece and nephew as well as a great-nephew and great-great-niece and I am sure that one day they will read her story and be surprised to learn more about their fearless, intrepid aunt.

Perhaps in compensation for not having children Herti has always been passionate about animals. For someone who is house-proud it is surprising to find her so welcoming of four-legged friends. Into the house they come with a welcome and Herti is soon on her knees having a good play. Children, too, are embraced with open arms. Herti loves my little 2-year-old granddaughter and the older ones are treated to drinks and biscuits, feeling at once comfortable and relaxed with this extraordinary woman. Recently my 15-year-old grandson called to fetch a ball that had gone over the hedge into her garden and was invited for refreshments and a lengthy chat.

In the middle of one of our sessions the phone rang. It was a lady who had recently moved about ten miles away and who had a sick dog. Could Herti drive her and the dog to the vet's hospital in Falmouth? 'Of course, I will help,' said Herti. She will respond to such a request and do whatever she can to help others. She is kind and thoughtful.

I try to imagine and build a picture of Herti as a teenager and young woman. The photos help but, in my mind, I see an energetic and physically fit girl with an alert expression, taking in everything in her surroundings. She isn't tall or statuesque – indeed she is petite, compact and slight. Wartime does not afford the opportunity to be fashion-conscious so as a teenager she wears school uniform and has a modest selection of 'out of school' clothes. A blouse, skirt, cardigan, ankle socks and sturdy shoes with a well-worn overcoat would have been the constituents of her wardrobe. I see her also in the uniform of the Hitler Youth carrying the swastika flag but I can clearly see beyond the surface to the true sentiments beneath this façade: Herti has no option but to comply with the demands of the Nazi invaders but inside she will never capitulate and knows that sometime she will have the chance to 'do her bit' for the war effort.

It was perhaps an unexpected step when Herti found herself progressing her career in the fashion and retail business, but I can see just how she would have adapted and proved so successful. Always a talented communicator, Herti would have been very effective at PR and customer relations. Her shrewd business sense enabled her to analyse where improvements could be made, and she was quick to put new strategies into place. Eventually, as post-war life began at last to show signs of prosperity, the shops were full of beautiful clothes and Herti needed no encouragement to take advantage of the chance to dress well and fashionably. To this day she is beautifully turned out, taking great pride in her appearance. In addition, being so 'good with people' enabled her to take the workforce with her and later, when working for British Airways, she was clearly gifted at making the customers feel both relaxed and satisfied. Of course, Herti's life continued to contain moments of high drama, even compared with her war experiences, and she recently told me about a couple of 'near misses' she had while working for BA. Once, when travelling in Kenya, the aircraft had a massive engine failure in the seconds before take-off but with great skill the pilot managed to abort the take-off and stop the aircraft safely. However, for political reasons the passengers were not allowed to disembark – there were South Africans on board who were in transit and could not set foot in Kenya – and were kept in the cabin for eight hours, during which time a pregnant woman gave birth. On another occasion, whilst working at Heathrow in 1984, Herti was on duty when a bomb exploded in the baggage hall immediately beneath her desk. Just on the other side of a hatchway a fellow worker was situated inside his office and he was practically blown through the small opening. A decade earlier, another explosion in the carpark area had blown the doors open, along with all the papers from Herti's desk and the pen from her hand. Yet again, Herti's response to these events was amazement that she had been so close to disaster but somehow had managed to avoid injury, or worse, and once more in her life had 'got away with it'.

Herti's house is adorned with some precious artworks that are a constant reminder of her happy times with her late husband, Doug. Together they enjoyed music, art and culture and in later years attended concerts in Truro. Nowadays Herti finds listening to the beautiful music she loved so much very difficult as the emotions it evokes make her feel sad rather than joyous: it is in Herti's nature to be happy and not to dwell on sadness so she avoids music and turns instead to other activities that help her to remain the optimistic, positive, open, cheerful, welcoming and delightful person that she is.

It has been a privilege to get to know Herti and to make a new friend. I hope that sharing her story and her determination to support the cause of morality and to resist oppression will give readers some insight into a remarkable person and help to remind us of the contribution made by so many during the past century to achieve the freedoms we enjoy today.

As I say, 'Goodbye, see you next week', Herti stands in her doorway waving and calling after me: 'I still can't believe I did those things! How on earth did I ever get away with it?'

Virginia Wells
Mullion, Summer 2019

*   *   *

My association with this particular work began in November 2019 when I was invited by Pen and Sword Books Ltd History commissions editor Claire Hopkins to join the project. My role was simply to build a chronological contextual framework around Herti's memoir, which had been created with the assistance of her good friend Virginia Wells. I planned to utilize material which I had at my disposal and which I had not used in any of my previous works to date. The sole aim was to build Herti's fascinating and valuable memoir into a full-length book and something which she and her family could be proud of. I can only add that it has been a great honour to have been asked to join this project and see it develop into the book it so deserved to be. Herti's story is far from being just another tale of a childhood under Nazism in the Second World War, but one of immense courage, morality, strength, humility, kindness and resourcefulness. I strongly believe that today, in the trying times in which we are now living, we can all learn something from the pages within this book and that we can all take something from it with which we can identify and apply to our own lives, especially in times of great adversity.

When I began my work on this book, I often thought of Herti's mother and father and what they would have made of their beloved daughter becoming an author so many decades after the end of the Second World War and at the grand old age of 90! Since the end of the Second World War Herti experienced many wonderful things in life which she was able to share with her mother and sister, Mädy. It is terribly sad that Herti's father was not able to share in these experiences and see his daughter flourish into the beautiful young woman that he would have been so proud of. The wonderful thing with Herti was that despite everything life threw at her and her family during those dark years of war, she endeavoured to fulfil her father's dying wish of looking after her mother and younger sister and honour the principles of her family life and upbringing. I think that having read this unique and evocative book, the reader will feel the same excitement, fear, joy, sadness and absolute admiration for Herti that I had from the moment I began reading what I believed to be one of the finest personal memoirs of the Second World War. With that said this is arguably one of the most important books from a personal perspective I have ever worked on and it has been an absolute honour and inspiration to have been involved in its creation.

Tim Heath
Evesham, November 2019

Prologue

I walk slowly along the narrow Cornish clifftop path, between Poldhu Cove and Polurrian, as I would do regularly with my lovely 10-year-old border collie, Mitzen. As usual, Mitzen is out in front, sniffing excitedly, his head held high and his nostrils taking in the fresh sea breeze. Whatever the weather, this lovely place reminds me of the beauty to be found in this world, wrapped in its kindness and benevolence. Far below, the surfers bob like black, shadowy seals amongst the waves, glistening in the golden light of late afternoon. Seabirds swoop and swerve around me. I am caught in the magic of the moment.

My mind wanders – walking the cliffs often made me contemplate the past and consider the great fortune I have enjoyed during my life. Here I am, entering my tenth decade, and amazed that I have not only survived this long but have, through luck and serendipity, overcome some of the great challenges of the twentieth century. My life has been shaped by the momentous upheaval that occurred in Europe and I am able to look back with gratitude to the many people who, through love, goodness and a sense of moral righteousness, took on the task of defeating evil and thus enabling me and so many others to enjoy the privilege of a long and happy life.

My second husband, Doug, and I moved to Cornwall after retiring in 1994. We had visited the Lizard Peninsula often over the years, always enjoying the contrast with the hectic pace of city life where I had worked for forty-four years and had had a very happy time and some interesting jobs. Together we spent eighteen good years exploring Devon and Cornwall and enjoying the contentment of living in a welcoming village community, walking the Cornish cliffs with our beloved dog and taking pleasure in the happy, loving life we had made. Here, relaxing in retirement, we made new friends and, together, continued to share new experiences and activities. Sadly, Doug passed away in 2012 and, not long after, I lost our much-loved dog. In spending the last few years living alone I have gradually reflected more and more on the events of my life, especially the war years: being so busy during my working life I gave little thought to these early years and yet they were so vital in shaping my future. I know that 'blanking out the past' is a tactic used by many people who experienced the horrors of war and only later do we feel the need to recall these events. Perhaps in this way it is possible to remind others of how important it is to learn from history, and this is why I feel a need to record my story. Also, as the recent commemorations of the 75th Anniversary of the D-Day landings and the final phases of the Second World War have highlighted, those of us who 'will never forget' our first-hand experiences are becoming fewer in number with each passing year, so it is important to record our stories before it is too late. I have been moved by the tales of heroism of the remaining nonagenarians and their emotional responses during the memorial services. My story may not be so dramatic but, in its own way, it tells of a young girl who saw an opportunity to do 'the right thing' and did not flinch from danger.

So, here I am, sitting alone in my comfortable home and, in my mind's eye, looking out towards the horizon, feeling wonderfully happy and wanting to hold on to this special moment in time. In my reverie, I lower myself onto the soft grass and immediately Mitzen stops and takes up his guarding position sitting upright in front of me, making sure I am safe. It is a warm afternoon and the sun is sinking in the west, the shadows of the surfers becoming darker. My mind floats back further to my childhood days in the beautiful Austrian countryside, where, on so many occasions, I would lie in the grass and start daydreaming, as I am at this moment.

Herti Bryan

Mullion, Cornwall – present day

Chapter 1

An Age of Innocence

Herti's early life and her memories of growing up in a loving family are especially vivid. As she revisits the past, the joy of recalling her happy childhood is evident in her expression and the details are as clear today as they were so long ago:

I was just three years old when my mother sent me on an errand to the corner shop. I remember looking back to see her smiling face as she watched me from the window. There are other glimpses of memory from the time we lived in this flat on the outskirts of Graz but in August 1932 we moved to a villa in another suburb of the city. Graz is a beautiful university city, in the south of Austria very near what is now the border with Slovenia, and I remember it as my tranquil home base for the early years of my life. To the north the mountains loomed: I remember hiking with my parents, having packed up my own little rucksack – off we would go in the early morning and return late in the afternoon or evening. We picked berries or mushrooms and occasionally would rescue injured animals. One young woodpigeon we nursed back to full health and, though it flew out of our garden eventually, it always returned to us and stayed for several years. In the winter it always snowed heavily – I would take my sleigh as far into the hills as I could manage and then enjoy a fast ride down the glistening slopes.

My early childhood was indeed idyllic. I was extremely happy and so blessed to have parents I adored and who loved me so much, as well as having wonderful grandparents, aunties and uncles who loved and spoilt me. As an only child I was very much indulged – we were such a close family and getting together for Easter and summer vacations were annual rituals that we all looked forward to. My parents and I would take the train from Graz to Mödling, before making the three-mile journey to Laxenburg, where my grandparents lived. Laxenburg was on the outskirts of Vienna and was where the Royal Palace was situated – a magnificent building set in beautiful parkland. My grandparents had a bakery – I can so easily recall the wonder of this place. My senses were overwhelmed by the amazing aromas coming from the hot ovens and it seemed I was surrounded by the most wonderful textures and tastes of delicious bread, rolls, cakes and confectionery. This was, indeed, heavenly.

Grandmother was truly 'grand' – an imposing Victorian figure who managed this thriving home and business with my grandfather. The bakery was renowned and successful meaning they could employ a number of permanent staff members as well as help in the house. There was a housekeeper, cook and stable boy who lived in accommodation at the back. In addition to the main house and bakery, there was a pigsty and a yard with geese and chickens. The stables housed the horses. My parents and I had our own room in the main house, but there was nothing I loved more than going to the adjoining shop to sample the delights on offer and to visit the bakery kitchen down the backstairs. Here I would watch as batches of bread were removed from the ovens on long poles. Often, I would be allowed to help with the bread making: I would be put in a high chair to reach the worktop and would do my best to knead the dough. Somehow my finished rolls were never as light, fluffy and good-looking as the professionally made ones but they tasted extra good to me and caused much fun and laughter.

Everyone at the Laxenburg house worked hard but it was always enjoyable and these were truly happy times. Grandmother served in the shop every morning but at 11 a.m. she would take her seat in her large, comfy armchair and ask Julie, the housekeeper, to bring her favourite zabaglione – a delicious dessert made from whisked egg yolks and sweet wine, served in a glass with dainty finger biscuits. She would invite me to share this treat with her, though my mother felt it inappropriate for a young child. Grandmother, however, thought a small amount of wine would do no harm so disregarded my mother's wishes and we shared our secret indulgence! To this day I enjoy making lovely zabaglione on special occasions and I will always choose it if it is on the dessert menu in a restaurant.

The bakery was extremely popular, not least because it was the only one for many miles around. Most of the bread was made during the night. At midnight my grandfather would start the process then, after a little sleep, he would get up again at 4 a.m. to continue. At 6 a.m. the bread was loaded onto carts and the daily deliveries would begin to the surrounding villages and towns and, as the Emperor's Summer Palace was close by, this important 'customer' was on the delivery round. There were very few cars or vans in the early 1930s so the journey by horse and cart was slow but soothing. I often accompanied my grandfather or uncle on their rounds, and, towards the end of the day, lulled by the gentle rhythm of the horse's hooves, we would fall asleep leaning against each other. Fortunately, the horse knew its way home and would return us safely to the house, pulling up in the stable yard behind the bakery.

However, when I was 5 years old, in 1934, my grandfather had a stroke and died. A year later my dear grandmother also died. Needless to say, the whole family was shocked by their loss – they had built the business into a very successful enterprise and had given our close-knit family a sound foundation. However, we carried on without them and my two uncles continued to run the bakery just as they always had and, amazingly, it has remained as a family business to this day. Though it was a tragedy to lose our beloved family members, in hindsight it was perhaps a good thing that neither of my grandparents ever had to hear the greeting 'Heil Hitler' as soldiers entered the shop or to witness the events of the next few years, which threw our lives into chaos.

About the same time that my grandparents died, I started school and I remember being very excited when the morning in September arrived for my first day. As the school was some distance from home, I travelled by tram in winter but always cycled when the warmer weather arrived. I loved school and learning so many new things. Every day was an adventure. I felt like a free spirit when cycling home, knowing that there would be more fun things to do with my family at home. I was truly blessed to have such loving parents and such a happy, secure home life – every day was special and I felt I was living in a fairy tale. In spite of the loss of my grandparents, my parents were able to show me – through their own strength – their powerful sense of commitment to each other and our family. I learnt from them the fundamental ideals that I have valued throughout my life and I have never doubted for a moment that these are the values that are worth fighting for.

I loved Sundays when my father, a police officer, was not on duty. In the mornings we would visit the cathedral in Graz city centre and listen to the beautiful music which, to this day, I regard as the best sound in the world. Afterwards, we would go to one of the many cafés and enjoy a leisurely coffee and a long chat. One of my favourite cafés was just a short walk from the cathedral and was situated on the first floor above an exclusive shop that sold luxury leather handbags and luggage. The café was beautifully furnished with soft red velvet seats. There would be a pianist playing and I would jump up to dance as soon as I heard it. The atmosphere was happy and lively, people laughed and applauded as I entertained them with my dancing – how could life be any more wonderful? I loved music so much that, when I was about 8, my parents bought me a baby grand piano and arranged for me to have private piano lessons. I practised hard and by the following Christmas had become quite proficient. After our Sunday morning special time together, Father and I would return home to a delicious meal lovingly prepared by my mother. In the afternoons we would often be joined by friends of my parents for a game of cards and Mother's fabulous home-baked cakes and coffee. By evening I was tired and ready for my comfy bed.

Each season held its special magic – life was full with so many things to do. In winter the snow fell for days on end which meant I would walk to school instead of going by tram. I recall the bright light of a snowy morning, the freezing cold, the fun of playing in the snow and sledging as well as the way the damp clumps of melting snow would thump as they fell from the rooftops or overhanging branches. Rushing home from school, I would snuggle by the log fire, listening to stories that my mother never tired of telling me while she sewed, making dresses and coats for me or keeping busy with some beautiful embroidery.

Christmas each year was celebrated in the traditional Austrian way. Whereas in the UK Father Christmas arrives during the night on Christmas Eve to deliver presents to well-behaved children, in Austria Santa visits during the early evening of 6 December. St Nicholas, dressed as Santa Claus, arrives accompanied by 'Krampus' who is dressed as a scary beast. These visitors come to each house and, if the children have been good, Santa Claus will hand out oranges, sweets and nuts which he carries in a huge sack. Krampus, on the other hand, will frighten any children who have misbehaved by chasing them with rusty chains and bells. How I dreaded the arrival of Krampus – until I realized that Santa had been told I had been a good girl again that year. In Austria children receive their main gifts on Christmas Eve rather than on Christmas Day. It is the belief that the 'Christkind' brings the presents to the children and puts them under the Christmas tree. The Christkind is a sprite-like child, usually depicted with blond hair and angelic wings. Clearly there is a similarity between the Christkind and the infant Jesus, whose birthday is to be celebrated, but sometimes it appears to be a specific angel bringing presents, which is often seen accompanying the image of baby Jesus in processions. Of course, children never actually see the Christkind and parents reinforce the message that presents are only brought to children who are not over-curious. When the parents say they think the Christkind may have visited, the whole family enters the living room together, where the Christmas tree has been decorated in readiness, for the opening of the presents – or *Bescherung*. Every year, I would spend Christmas Eve with my aunties in town whilst my parents decorated a very large tree and arranged the presents. I could scarcely wait to get home, full of excitement and anticipation of the joys that would greet me. As there was no public transport after midday on Christmas Eve, we would eagerly trudge back through the snow, in a magical, wonderful, silent world lit only by the starry sky which we would gaze at, searching for a glimpse of the Christkind flying towards my house. Arriving home, we entered the welcoming warmth. My parents opened the door to the living room and there was the Christmas tree, glistening with real candles and decorated with biscuits and sweets wrapped in pretty paper. Underneath the branches were the presents and, oh what a joy it was to discover the treasures that were there each year. I would rush quickly to the piano and play 'Silent Night', my aunties and parents singing along – this was the true beginning of another wonderful Christmas. Then it was time for a light fish supper and a play with my presents before bedtime. Christmas Day itself was a quiet family day when I would play with my new toys and mother would cook a delicious dinner. The next day we would go to a traditional children's matinée theatrical performance. How I adored these Christmases and the memories of such happy times come flooding back in my mind as each new Christmas comes around. But, as we celebrated Christmas and welcomed the New Year of 1938, little did we know just how drastically our lives were about to change in a matter of a few months.

Chapter 2

A Dark Omen

In the wake of the First World War the former Austro-Hungarian Empire was effectively dissolved in favour of the state of Austria, comprising the largely German-speaking peoples of the former empire. Austria became constituted as a parliamentary democracy, the two dominant political elements in Austria at that time being the socialists represented by the Social Democratic Workers Party and Conservatives represented by the Christian Social Party. Naturally, the SDWP gained a major portion of support from the working-class areas of Austria's cities, while the Conservatives built on the support of the rural populations and the upper classes. The Conservatives also maintained a close alliance with the Roman Catholic Church which had some of the country's leading clerics within its ranks.

Mirroring most of the nascent European democracies of the time, politics in Austria began to embrace a highly ideological thesis. Both the socialist and conservative movements were far more than merely political parties: both possessed far-ranging power structures, which included their own independent paramilitary forces. For example, the Conservatives formed the Heimwehr (Homeguard) in 1921–1923 and, in direct retaliation, the Social Democrats created paramilitaries called the Republikanischer Schutzbund (Republican Protection Association) after 1923. In a chilling similarity to the social and political events which would later tear Germany apart, violence would break out between these two forces especially at political rallies.

The first major confrontation involving these paramilitary groups took place in early 1927, when members of the Hermann Hiltl's Frontkämpfervereinigung (Front Fighters Union – a group affiliated with the Conservative camp) shot and killed an 8-year-old boy and a war veteran marching with the Schutzbund in a peaceful counter-demonstration in Schattendorf, a town in the district of Mattersburg, in the Austrian state of Burgenland. In July, three defendants in the court case which followed were acquitted, which led to outrage in the left-wing camp. On 15 July 1927, a general strike occurred, and demonstrations took place in the capital. Trouble rapidly broke out and, following the storming of a police station, security forces began opening fire upon demonstrators. An angry mob then set fire to the Justizpalast (palace of Justice) in response to the indiscriminate shooting. The reason this building was targeted was the fact it was viewed by many as a symbol of a flawed and partial judicial system. Altogether, 89 people lost their lives in this outbreak of violence (85 of the victims being demonstrators) in what became known as the July Revolt and hundreds of others were injured. Strangely, the violence abated rapidly, and the quarrelling factions took their fight back into the political arena and off the streets.

This was by no means the end of the First Republic's problems which seemed to worsen with each coming year. The Great Depression which blighted world society from 1929 well into the 1930s hit Austria hard. As with Germany the effects of high rates of unemployment, particularly among the poor and working classes, combined with hyperinflation would prove disastrous for many. In order to define the effects of hyperinflation upon a country like Austria one should imagine a basic everyday commodity such as a loaf of bread which, virtually overnight, became unaffordable to many. Austria's paper currency, as in Germany, became so worthless that it was often used in place of coal to burn on fires. This hyperinflation was the catalyst for mass social discontent which would have far-reaching consequences for Austria as an independent nation.

Austria's association with Adolf Hitler's Third Reich was formed over the months following the Austrian civil war. In reality, it was hardly a civil war within the usual context, but more a series of skirmishes which took place between 12 and 16 February 1934. The skirmishes came in the form of pitched battles between the two opposing political ideologies of fascism and socialism. The troubles began in Linz, soon spreading to the cities of Vienna, Graz, Bruck an der Mur, Judenburg, Wiener Neustadt and Steyr. Trouble also flared up in some of the industrial cities of eastern and central Austria.

*   *   *

Herta Juliana Bryan (née Krause) was born on 21 February 1929 in the city of Graz, the second largest city in Austria. Her parents were Karl Krause, born on 15 August 1893 in Krieglach, Styria, and Anna Krause (née Busch), born on 1 September 1902 in Pfaffstatten, Lower Austria. One of Herti's early recollections of her pre-Anschluss life in Austria was of the troubles which flared in February 1934. Herti recalls:

A hint of things to come occurred in 1934 when I was about 5 years old. I had been playing on my tricycle in the garden one sunny morning when I heard loud banging noises. Immediately my mother called me into the house and we both sat behind a door, aware that guns were being fired around us. Frightened, we clung to one another as the bullets ricocheted off the surrounding walls. Gradually the gunfire diminished and after about an hour (though it seemed longer) it stopped completely. When Father arrived home, anxious about our welfare though unaware of exactly what had been happening to us, he was so relieved to find us safe and unharmed. I learned later that this was a failed coup d'état by the Austrian Nazis, and, though quickly suppressed, it was to foreshadow future events.

Several hundred people including paramilitaries, members of the security forces and civilians lost their lives in this brief yet violent conflict, with over a thousand suffering wounds of varying degrees. The Austrian authorities were anxious that no such uprising should be allowed to occur again: subsequently the punishments administered to those convicted of having taken part in the troubles were justly severe. The authorities put on trial and executed nine Schutzbund (Austrian paramilitary organization) leaders under the provisions of martial law. American journalist and author John Gunther reported that Schutzbund members received what he termed 'mercilessly severe' sentences. In addition, over 1,500 arrests were made. Prominent Socialist political leaders such as Otto Bauer, an Austrian Social Democrat, were forced into exile. Bauer was considered one of the leading thinkers of the left-socialist Austro–Marxist grouping. Bauer was also an inspirational figure for both the New Left and Eurocommunist movements whose aim was to find a 'Third Way' to democratic socialism.

In the wake of the troubles the Austrian government acted quickly to prohibit the Social Democratic Party and its affiliated trade unions altogether. In May the Conservatives replaced the democratic constitution with a corporatist constitution modelled along the lines of Benito Mussolini's Fascist Italy; thus, the socialists coined the phrase 'Austrofascism' although the underlying ideology was essentially that of the most conservative elements within the Austrian Catholic clergy, a feature inconsistent with both Italian Fascism and Nazism. The Vaterländische Front, or Fatherland Front, was the ruling political organization of Austrofascism. The ethos of this Fatherland Front claimed it to be a non–partisan movement with the sole aim of uniting all the people of Austria, overcoming all political and social divisions in the country. The Fatherland Front was fully aligned with the Catholic Church and did not advocate any racial ideology, as would the later Italian Fascism. It advocated principally Austrian nationalism and independence from Germany on the basis of protecting Austria's Catholic religious identity from what many Austrians felt was a Protestant-dominated German state.

The Heimwehr (Home Guard), the nationalist paramilitary group operating within Austria during the 1920s and 1930s in much the same way as the Freikorps in Germany, and the Christian Social Party were merged into the Fatherland Front, becoming the only legal political party in the resulting authoritarian regime – the Ständestaat or corporate state.

Adolf Hitler's desires towards his birthplace of Austria had been made clear within the first part of the text of his book, *Mein Kampf* (*My Struggle*), which Hitler had written during his period of incarceration following the failed putsch of 1924. In his book Hitler wrote of Austria: 'German Austria must return to the great German motherland' and 'Common blood belongs in a common Reich'. There could be no illusion as to Hitler's intention of reclaiming Austria for Germany as part of his Third Reich. Yet, Hitler's geographical aspirations in Europe stretched far beyond Germany's immediate neighbours.

It is a more than obvious fact that Adolf Hitler's Nazi ideology had been greatly influenced by the brand of fascism created by Italian dictator Benito Mussolini. Italy was the birthplace of fascism as we understand it. Mussolini would enjoy a twenty-one-year 'dance with the devil', ruling Italy from 1922 until 1943. Encompassing the same nationalistic desires as Hitler, Mussolini had not only planned to restore Italian territories but to expand upon them, a course of action deemed necessary for a nation to assert its superiority and strength in order to avoid falling into political and social decay. Mussolini and the Italian Fascists believed that Italy was the heir to ancient Rome and its legacy. Thus, the principle of the creation of a new Italian empire in which *Spazio Vitale* or 'living space' for the Italian people would be created, along with the control of the Mediterranean Sea: this concept proved to be an attractive proposition to many Italians at the time. Imitation being the sincerest form of flattery, one can now clearly see the similarities between the Nazi fascist ideology and that embraced by the Italians. Both were espoused through the same principles of racial superiority, hatred, anti-Semitism and the restriction of the basic freedoms and rights of a society to self-determination through democratic means.

Although Italy and the fledgling Nazi Germany were some years away from their political and military alliance, both were representative of the troubles that had blighted Europe from the mid-1920s through to the 1930s. Political and social chaos, economic depression, mass unemployment and borderline starvation were all the factors required for fascism to become the perceived acceptable means to an end.

* * *

Hanna Ahrens, a young Austrian housewife who lived in the market town of Lustenau, wrote a letter to a friend living in London, England, in 1937 about what she described as a 'gathering storm' throughout parts of Europe at the time. In fact, Hanna never sent the letter and it was amongst personal possessions inherited by her granddaughter, Ingrid Hoess. Ingrid recalled the discovery of the letter and its contents:

> It was written in a fearful hand; my grandmother wrote as if she were prophesying some terrible coming event. She wrote of a world that was slowly going mad, where in Germany a great evil was rising and taking hold of a people who should know better than to embrace this. She had witnessed this madness spread from Germany into Austria and she had the uneasy feeling that it was just a matter of time before Germany's new leader, Adolf Hitler, would claim her country as his own. Hitler's rhetoric was full of hatred and loathing, vowing to wreak vengeance and take back what was rightfully his. My grandmother understood what his brand of national community meant for Austria. As a primarily German-speaking nation, there would be no escape from this man or his desires to supposedly unite the German people once again. My grandmother wrote: 'It would be a unity

bound with the spilling of the blood of the innocent. It was as if the fuse to a stick of dynamite had been lit and could not be snuffed out. No one dared to throw any water upon it, no one was brave enough to drag the naughty little boy out of the class and give him the thrashing he so deserved. It felt like the whole world had suddenly lost its way, its sense of right and wrong and its conscience. Dark clouds are gathering, and war feels as if it is coming.'

Ingeborg Nietzer was a 13-year-old schoolgirl and she remembered vividly the feeling of Austrian society in the weeks leading up to the *Anschluss*:

There was this strange sense of both fear and excitement. There was this view that if the Germans came, we would all be so much stronger, that unity with the Germans was a logical cause. Yet at the same time there were many that wanted that separate identity as Austrians, people who felt we should remain independent of Germany, people who were proud of being Austrian. People were saying, 'the Germans will be here soon, then this person had better watch out or that person had better watch out.' It was, in many ways, a sign of what was to come, that people with scores to settle would welcome the Germans. We knew of the racial policies that existed in Germany and we knew that there were people who lived among us who would be in danger if the Germans came. I felt for some of my school friends as I knew some of them had Jewish ancestry. Some of us at the time just hoped it would go away, that it would never happen, but sadly we were wrong. The Germans wouldn't leave us alone and they were going to invade us. However, it would be an invasion welcomed by the majority of our society and those who welcomed the Nazis into our country must shoulder the greater portion of blame for all that happened afterwards in our country.

Anders Bilch, who was Swedish by birth, had worked in Vienna for many years, leaving just two months prior to the Anschluss. Anders wrote of the situation:

> This Hitler individual is much like a cat sniffing around a mousehole. He understands that both fear and lies are the greatest weapon one can use against another human being. He surrounds himself with his legions, dressed in brown and black, professing [himself] to be the saviour of the Germanic peoples. If this man is indeed to be the saviour of Germany, then may God help them, and may God help us all.

The above words written now so long ago were at the time of their writing a prophecy of fear and darkness, of a world seemingly unwilling to prevent the inevitable catastrophe it was now heading towards. Whilst Austria was composed largely of ethnic German-speaking people, many Austrians expressed a wish to remain independent of German rule. However, it is a sad irony that Austria would, within a short period of time, fall under the dark shadow of Adolf Hitler's Third Reich. It is certainly true that, even at this time of great uncertainty in Europe, had the greater powers of Britain and the United States taken action, they could, potentially, have curtailed Adolf Hitler's desires in conquering Western Europe. America was unwilling to become involved in what it termed another war in Europe and many political leaders in the United States held the view that Adolf Hitler was Europe's problem and not a concern of the USA. Russia, under Josef Stalin, was content with waiting in the side-lines for any geographical 'crumbs' in the east that Hitler might throw his way, and it appeared that Britain and France were ill-prepared to confront such a powerful military force at that particular time. There are those who argue that one solution lay in the assassination of Hitler himself. It is feasible that had Hitler been assassinated Germany may well have once again collapsed into political and social discontent and would have, at least temporarily, been distracted from its path towards war. The problem with any proposed assassination, as history proves, is the fact that Hitler would, in all probability, have only been succeeded by another sycophant within the regime with much the same ambition. Historians estimate that at least forty-two plots were made against the life of Adolf Hitler and, of those that were carried out, all failed. It certainly appeared that Hitler had some form of uncanny luck on his side and that the outbreak of full-scale war was now an inevitability that the world was powerless to prevent.

Chapter 3

Anschluss

On 12 March 1938, German troops marched into Austria in what was to become known as the *Anschluss* (annexation of Austria). There was no gunfire, no blood-curdling scream of Stukas overhead nor the rumble of tanks and artillery. The Anschluss was no *Blitzkrieg*: on the contrary many Austrians from all backgrounds welcomed the Germans and the union of Austria and Germany which followed. Many Austrian citizens felt that this union was a logical progression in bringing ethnic Germans outside of Nazi Germany into the fold of a Greater Germany. Nazi Germany had provided assistance to the Austrian National Socialist Party (Austrian Nazi Party) in its bid to seize power from the Austrian Fatherland Front government, as outlined in the previous chapter. In a conversation with Nazi propaganda minister, Joseph Goebbels, in the late summer of 1937, Adolf Hitler confided that eventually Austria would have to be taken 'by force'.

On 5 November 1937, Hitler convened a conference with the Foreign Minister Konstantin von Neurath, the War Minister Field Marshal Werner von Blomberg, Army commander General Werner von Fritsch, Kriegsmarine commander Admiral Erich Raeder and Luftwaffe commander Hermann Göring. At this conference Hitler stated that economic problems were causing Germany to fall behind in the arms race with Britain and France and that the only solution was to launch, in the near future, a series of wars to seize Austria and Czechoslovakia, whose resources could be utilized to benefit Germany in the arms race. In early 1938, Hitler was seriously considering replacing Papen as ambassador to Austria with either Colonel

Hermann Kriebel, the German consul in Shanghai, or Albert Forster, the Gauleiter of Danzig. Ironically, neither Kriebel nor Forster were professional diplomats. Kriebel had been one of the leaders of the failed 1923 Munich Beer Hall Putsch. He had been appointed consul in Shanghai to facilitate his work in arms procurement and dealing in China. Forster on the other hand was a Gauleiter who had proven he could get along with the Poles within his position in the Free City of Danzig. Both men were committed Nazis who had displayed some diplomatic qualities. On 25 January 1938, the Austrian police raided the Vienna headquarters of the Austrian Nazi Party, arresting Gauleiter Leopold Tavs, the deputy to Captain Josef Leopold, discovering a cache of weapons and plans for a putsch.

Following increasing threats of violence and demands from Hitler that Austria agree to a union with Germany, Austrian Chancellor Kurt Schuschnigg met Hitler at Berchtesgaden on 12 February 1938, in an effort to avoid the takeover of Austria. Hitler presented Schuschnigg with a series of demands that included appointing Nazi sympathizers to positions of power within the Austrian government. The key appointment out of all of this was that of Arthur Seyss-Inquart as Minister of Public Security. Within this role Seyss-Inquart would possess unlimited control of the Austrian police. In return Hitler would publicly reaffirm his support for Austria's national sovereignty. Schuschnigg, browbeaten and threatened by Hitler, agreed to these demands and put them into effect.

Seyss-Inquart was a long-time supporter of the Nazis who sought the union of all German people into a single state. Leopold argued that he was a moderate who favoured an evolutionary approach to union. He opposed the violent tactics the Austrian Nazis favoured, cooperated with Catholic groups, and wanted to preserve a measure of Austrian identity within Nazi Germany.

On 20 February, Hitler made a speech before the Reichstag which was broadcast live and which for the first time was relayed also by the Austrian Radio network. A key phrase in Hitler's speech, which was primarily aimed at the Germans living in Austria and Czechoslovakia, was 'The German Reich is no longer willing to tolerate the suppression of ten million Germans across its borders'.

On 9 March 1938, in the face of rioting by the small, yet virulent, Austrian Nazi Party and ever-increasing German demands on Austria, Chancellor Schuschnigg reluctantly called a referendum on the issue to be held on 13 March. Hitler was furious upon hearing this news and threatened to invade Austria demanding that Schuschnigg resign and Seyss-Inquart take his place. Hitler's thinking was that Seyss-Inquart could call for the immediate assistance of the German armed forces who would then rush to Austria's aid, restoring order and giving what was, in fact, an invasion the feel of legitimacy in the eyes of the world. In the face of this threat, Schuschnigg informed Seyss-Inquart that the referendum would be cancelled.

Chancellor Schuschnigg was rapidly 'swimming out of his depth' within the political situation he was now facing. Although a public vote on the issue of unification was suggested by Schuschnigg, it was clear that Hitler would not stand by while Austria declared its will to be independent through a public vote. Hitler declared that any such action would be subject to fraud and that Germany would never accept the outcome. In addition to this the German propaganda ministry began to 'spin' press reports of rioting breaking out in Austria and that large parts of Austrian society were calling for German troops to enter the country to restore order. Schuschnigg countered that all reports of rioting were false.

Hitler, becoming increasingly irritated with the situation, sent an ultimatum to Schuschnigg on 11 March, demanding that he hand over all power to the Austrian Nazis or face an invasion by German forces. This ultimatum was to expire at noon but was extended by two hours. Without waiting for a response from the Chancellor, Hitler had already signed the order to send German troops into Austria at one o'clock. Yet even at this stage it appeared that Hitler had greatly underestimated his opposition.

Edgar Ansel Mowrer, a reporter for CBS News who was in Paris at the time, recalled: 'There is no one in all France who does not believe that Hitler invaded Austria not to hold a genuine plebiscite, but to prevent the plebiscite planned by Schuschnigg from demonstrating to the entire world just how little hold National Socialism really had on that tiny country.'

Schuschnigg valiantly sought support for Austrian independence through the hours following the ultimatum. It soon became apparent that neither Britain nor France was going to offer any assistance. Under these circumstances Schuschnigg resigned on the evening of 11 March. However, President Wilhelm Miklas refused to appoint Seyss-Inquart as the new Chancellor. At 8.45 p.m. Hitler, who had been pacing much like an angry beast within a cage, grew tired of waiting and ordered the invasion of Austria to commence at dawn on 12 March regardless of the situation as it may be. At around 10 p.m. that evening a counterfeit telegram was sent in Seyss-Inquart's name requesting the assistance of German troops, since he was not yet Chancellor and was unable to do so himself. Seyss-Inquart was not installed as Chancellor until after midnight, when Miklas resigned himself to the inevitable. In a radio broadcast in which he announced his resignation, he argued that he accepted the changes and allowed the Nazis to take over the government 'to avoid the shedding of fraternal blood'. Seyss-Inquart was appointed Chancellor shortly after midnight on 12 March.

Hitler was not happy with the current situation, pouring scorn on those journalists and reporters who failed to agree with his actions towards Austria. As Hitler listened to Bruckner's Seventh Symphony on his gramophone, he stood up and remarked, 'How can anyone say that Austria is not German! Is there anything more German than our old, pure Austrianness?'

On the morning of 12 March, the German Wehrmacht crossed the border into Austria. There was no hostility, only joy and the German troops were greeted by cheering Austrians who gave Nazi salutes, waved small Nazi flags bearing the swastika and showered them with flowers.

Little did the Austrian people realize that this uncontested invasion of their country was the first big test for the Wehrmacht which was, in fact, not only badly organized but poorly coordinated too. This mattered very little since the Austrian government had ordered its Bundesheer (Austrian Armed Forces) not to resist the Germans. It is entirely feasible that had the Bundesheer resisted they may well have temporarily thwarted the German invasion of their country.

In the afternoon of that fateful day Adolf Hitler, accompanied by a 4,000-strong bodyguard, crossed the border into Austria at his birthplace of Braunau am Inn. Clearly elated at taking Austria without a shot being fired, Hitler waved to the crowds who had begun to gather. Some Austrian citizens stood in bemused silence, others cheered and gave the Nazi salute, while there were some who stood with their heads in their hands and cried. Whether the latter were tears of joy or fear was difficult to ascertain at that time. By nightfall Hitler had arrived at Linz where he was given an enthusiastic welcome. The level of enthusiasm displayed towards the invading Germans surprised both Nazis and non-Nazis, as many were of the view that a majority of Austrian citizens opposed Anschluss. The reality was that a large proportion of Germans from both Austria and Germany itself viewed the Anschluss as a long-overdue unification of the German people, who were now united within a single German state. Hitler had originally intended to leave Austria as a puppet state with Seyss-Inquart as head of a pro-Nazi government. Such was the overwhelming reception to the German invasion that he had a change of heart and made the decision to absorb Austria into the Reich. From this moment on Austria was no longer an independent state but a 'mechanic' of the Third Reich.

Ingeborg Nietzer recalls the German invasion:

There was no fighting and the German troops were greeted as liberating heroes. There were women standing at the roadsides handing out flowers to the Germans as they marched past and some ran up to the soldiers to kiss them on the cheek. When I first saw the Germans, I was amazed by how smart and disciplined they appeared in their uniforms. Their black boots were polished and shone in the sunlight and some had their medals pinned to their tunics. Many of the soldiers wore Iron Crosses – a symbol of bravery in battle. As they marched past many were smiling and probably feeling very proud of themselves. There was this brief period of calm under the German occupation which lasted for a week or so and then the violence started. I often visited the nearby town with my friends on a Saturday morning. We were doing the things that many kids did back then, buying sweets and playing and having fun. I remember well the violence the Nazis brought with them. One Saturday morning, my friends and I witnessed a family being dragged from their home. It was an awful spectacle: there were two young men, three kids, an elderly gentleman and two young women. They were being bundled into the back of a military lorry. The old man was struggling to get up into the vehicle so two of the Germans jumped down from the back of the lorry, beat the old man and then threw him into the back of the lorry. While this was happening one of the kids, a young boy, made a run for it. He ran like a hare and almost made it until one of the Germans aimed his rifle and fired. The boy fell and rolled along the ground where he lay still. One of the Germans then went and grabbed the dead boy by the scruff and dragged him to the back of the lorry before throwing him in like a dead animal or something. The others were screaming and crying as the lorry drove off. We stood and listened to their cries as they became faint in the distance. Being young people, we were curious, so we walked to the spot where the boy had fallen dead and looked down at the pool of blood on the ground. We asked local people why had these people been taken away. We were curtly told to 'mind our own business', that it was 'nothing to do with you', and to 'bugger off'! Violence and murder became a defining feature of that dreadful regime. We wanted no part in it, but what choices did we have? Who was going to come and rescue us? No one! My parents were terrified of the Nazis, although since they were both 'pure Austrian' they had little to fear from them. My parents used to warn me, 'You do as you are told, obey them and don't ever upset or defy them.'

Herti Bryan recalled vividly the events of that day back in March of 1938 when the country she loved fell under the Hitler spell:

It was March 1938 and I was just 9 years old. Mother and I sat listening to the news on the radio in the kitchen. Father was getting ready to go to work, dressing in his police uniform. Chancellor Kurt Schuschnigg was talking to the nation about the threat that Austria would soon be invaded by Hitler's troops. He told us that he did not want this to happen but felt it would be better for Austria to surrender and to become a part of the German Third Reich, rather than to resist which would inevitably lead to defeat. Thus the Anschluss began as Austria lost its autonomy and came under the rule of Germany and Hitler increased his stranglehold on Europe.

We were horrified. I'll never forget Mother's face as she absorbed the terrible news. Father continued to prepare for work, but he was quiet and had a look of anxiety and uncertainty. The happy idyll of my childhood was shaken badly – we knew for sure that life was going to be very different and we had no idea just what the future would hold. We had questions spinning in our heads for which there were no answers. The image of this scene remains clearly as one of those moments that one simply knows is going to be momentous. My parents were devastated – the tone of their conversations changed as it did for everyone in the community. Everywhere there was tension and anxiety in the air. We waited …

Nothing much happened. I went to school and continued to enjoy my studies as I started my final year of primary school. Father went to work as usual. We went to Laxenburg for our holidays where I enjoyed all the usual pleasures of life at the bakery. However, one couldn't help but notice the increasing military presence in the area. Of course, the Emperor's Palace had attracted the attention of the Nazis and, being such a luxurious and spacious building, they had requisitioned it for billeting a company of SS soldiers. Naturally, being close to Vienna where there were many Jews living, this provided a convenient point from which to round up the many Jews in the city and surrounding villages and towns. I remember on one occasion noticing, as I looked out of the bakery window, a number of large open-topped trucks driving past. They stopped outside in the main road leading down to the Emperor's Palace. Next, I saw a crowd of old people and younger adults being marched along and loaded onto the vehicles. All these people wore a yellow Star of David on the backs of their coats. I didn't know what to make of this – everyone was anxious about it and Mother told me not to be seen looking out of the window. We knew these people were going somewhere – but we didn't know where. Later, life went on as normal: I rode my bicycle and played with my friends. The summer passed and another winter came, along with the excitement of Christmas – just the same as always. Only much later did I hear these poor souls had been taken to concentration camps.

Gradually more changes were happening. One day my father came home in a completely different uniform – one he was now required to wear. Gone was his Austrian police uniform and in its place was the dress worn by the German police. Into our house came Nazi insignia of various kinds – our national identity was being eroded and a new one was being imposed.

Then there was the scrutiny of my father's suitability to be a member of this new police force: he was required to prove the purity of his race by providing evidence that there was no Jewish blood in his ancestry, going back several generations on both sides of the family. As it happens, his bloodline was 'pure' though I have often wondered what would have become of our family had this not been the case. I was only too aware that some of my classmates were suddenly no longer at school: one day we would have been playing happily together as usual and the next they simply had gone. It was not difficult to make the connection between their disappearance and their Jewish racial status, but we had no idea of why they had left or, indeed, where they gone. I just knew that I missed my friends and was worried about their fate.

One afternoon I was sitting with my mother by the window – she was sewing, and I was doing my homework. A large black car drew up outside our neighbours' house. Two Gestapo officers, dressed in long, black leather overcoats and hats, got out and marched to the front door. Without waiting for the door to be opened they entered the house. Moments later we witnessed our neighbours, named Roschitz – a lovely couple – being dragged out of the house by the Gestapo men and bundled into the car. Fortunately, their new and much-loved baby was left behind in the house with his grandmother who just happened to be visiting – this little child had been desperately 'wanted' and the parents had waited many years to be blessed with their son. Tragically, we found out much later that the father was taken to Dachau concentration camp and the mother to Auschwitz where they were both killed. For more than eight decades I have wondered whatever happened to the little boy – whether he is still living, and what he knew about his parents' fate. I think how good fortune enabled me to survive and enjoy future happiness – in spite of his tragic early loss, was he lucky enough to survive the war and did his life have a good outcome?

The campaign of terror against Jews in Austria began with immediate effect following the Anschluss. In scenes reminiscent of those occurring in Germany itself, Jews were systematically rounded up by the Nazi authorities. Jewish-owned shops and homes were looted with property and possessions being confiscated; Jews were beaten up in the streets before being forced to wash away pro-independence slogans daubed on the streets ahead of the failed 13 March plebiscite. Jewish actresses from the Theatre in der Josefstadt were seized by members of the SA (Brownshirts, the Nazi paramilitary organization) and were then forced to clean toilets. It was reported by several sources that the SA thugs assaulted the women, even forcing their heads into the lavatories. The process of Aryanization took place very rapidly in Austria. Within a few months Jews or anyone with Jewish ancestry were driven out of public life. The disappearing school friends that Herti recalls in the wake of the Anschluss are stark testimony to the Nazi brutality that was now taking place in Austria. These children had most likely been unfortunate enough to have had Jewish ancestry or they may have had some physical impediment which, under the Hitler Youth law, would have almost certainly condemned them as 'unfit Aryans'. Either way, from what we know and understand of the Nazi racial mechanics it is very likely that at least some of these unfortunate young souls perished in one of the many camps instituted for this very purpose.

Herti has in her possession a photograph of her class, at Hasnerplatz School, taken on 11 June – this was possibly to mark the final day of the school year. It shows twenty girls in her class and her teacher, Professor Wilhemine Krainer, who was with the class for four years, throughout Herti's time in primary school. The names of all the children and the teacher are written on the reverse and the photograph is reproduced in the images section of this book. It is uncertain if the picture was taken in 1938 or 1939 and it has been difficult for Herti to remember such details precisely. At some point, someone has identified nine of the girls with a cross, but Herti does not know for sure who did this or what it indicates. She assumed that the crosses marked girls who 'disappeared' but it could simply be an indication of which school they were going on to after primary school – some to the grammar school with Herti and some to the Hauptschule (secondary modern equivalent). In any case, Herti knows without doubt that her friend, Lori Reichenfelser, marked with a cross, wrote a message in Herti's autograph book on 26 March 1941, proving she was 'alive and well' at that date. After so many years it may not be possible to track down these children to ascertain their fate – and it may well be that whoever marked the photograph did so in retrospect to identify girls who did, indeed, 'disappear'. What we do know is that Herti definitely recalls that some children in her class simply vanished overnight and some of these girls will, in all probability, have been victims of Hitler's racial 'elimination' policy.

The names given on the reverse of the photograph are as follows, left to right:

Back row: Helga Tragan*, Traude Sewanno, Inge Lyckowetz*, Etta Schönecker, Erika Schwarz

Middle row: Silvya Baiterer, Mitzie Kuschel*, Inge Kutzma, Herta Krause, Susi Baldinester, Greta Kubkat*, Elfi Kainz, Lori Reichenfelser*

Front row: Heidi Mühlbacher*, Traudi Haucink*, Irma Hauer, Dorli Birnick, Gretl Leibgret*, Gerta Nienaus*, Christa Rumpf.

For me (Tim Heath), this was a particularly harrowing part of Herti's memoir, so much so that I commissioned my friend and fellow Pen and Sword author, Annamarie Vickers, to write a poem dedicated to the memory of all the children who were taken by the Nazis and who suffered the horrors of the concentration and death camps. The poem, 'In the Arms of Angels', follows:

In the Arms of Angels

Nobody told me, we were playing hide and seek
But they must have changed the rules as they've been gone all
   week.
Empty desks in the classroom and nobody says a word
I feel them out there, screaming,
But still they can't be heard

Maybe if I count to ten my friends may reappear
From the darkest corner imaginable
Suddenly they'll be here
Searching these corridors of pain
Calling out your names
Hoping one day soon
That I will see your faces again.

Innocent school children cruelly taken away
Yet to realize that this wasn't just an ordinary day
Lost souls searching desperately for the light
Baby sparks of energy that deserved to shine so bright.

Safe now in the arms of angels
Away from hurt and pain
Free from judgement caused by the blood flowing in their veins
At one with Mother Nature
Little whispers on the breeze
Sleep now, little ones
You can finally be at peace.

When studying the Third Reich today, one should never forget the
devastating human impact, the outright murder and the destruction
that this regime was responsible for.

The violence against Jews in Austria came to its horrific climax over 9/10 November 1938 during what became known as the Kristallnacht (Night of Broken Glass) pogrom. The Nazis destroyed all the synagogues and prayer houses in Vienna and violence and destruction erupted in towns and cities all over Austria. The only Jewish synagogue to have survived the torch was the Stadttempel which had been built within a residential area and it was this fact that prevented it from being burned down by the Nazi mobs. During the course of Kristallnacht over 6,000 Jews were arrested, the majority being immediately processed and sent to the Dachau concentration camp.

The Nuremberg Laws, which came into effect in Austria from May 1938, were reinforced with innumerable anti-Semitic decrees. Jews were gradually robbed of their freedom, blocked from virtually every profession, excluded from schools and universities and – from September 1941 – were forced to wear the Yellow Badge, as it was known. This yellow badge was the Star of David that all Jews would have to wear. The Nazis dissolved Jewish organizations and institutions in the hope that many thousands of Jews would emigrate. To an extent this plan worked as, by the end of 1941, 130,000 Jews had left Vienna, 30,000 of whom went to the United States. Most of this number had left virtually everything that they owned behind, yet were forced to pay the Reich Flight Tax placed upon all émigrés from Nazi Germany. Some Jews were able to obtain support from international aid organizations so they could pay this tax. These were, however, the fortunate ones, as the majority of Jews who chose to remain behind in Vienna or had no means to leave would eventually become victims of the Holocaust. It seemed hypocritical that while the Nazis wanted Jews to be evicted from the territories they had claimed as their own, they made it very difficult for many to do so. Of the 65,000 Viennese Jews who were subsequently deported to the concentration camps, fewer than 2,000 survived.

Herti continues:

It was indeed very hard for us to comprehend the 'ethnic cleansing' that was occurring all around us. More and more of the people we had known as good friends, neighbours or simple acquaintances were just disappearing. We had never really considered their 'Jewishness', their race or religion – these were members of our community and we could not understand the ideology of removing them from all that was familiar to them, the confiscation of their possessions and the compulsory relocation to places we had no concept of. When visiting Laxenburg, I witnessed SS officers coming into the bakery to buy bread. They were smart and always formal, clicking their heels and offering the Nazi greeting, which the shop assistants would do their best to quietly ignore. However, it was difficult to reconcile these seemingly polite officers with the black-coated, armed thugs we had witnessed dragging our neighbours away and other such dreadful events that were becoming more commonplace. We knew that bad things were happening but were powerless to respond in any way. As a 9-year-old only child, I missed the school friends who had so mysteriously disappeared and was feeling particularly lonely, in spite of my loving family and many relatives. For years I had longed for a baby brother or sister, and now the idea of a new life in the family seemed more important than ever: how I wished that the 'stork' would bring a baby to our family! In Austrian folklore it was necessary to tempt the 'stork' with sugar put on the windowsill every evening and this I did regularly in the hope I would be rewarded with a new addition to our family. One day I went to the letterbox to collect the post and noticed a card addressed to me. On one side was a picture of a stork carrying a sling in its beak which cradled a baby! On the reverse the message read: 'Thank you for the sugar and I promise I will bring you a sister or brother, but it will take some time as I am in Spain at the moment'! I was so excited and could scarcely wait for the day to arrive when our new baby was 'delivered'. On 28 February 1939 my little sister Annemarie "Mädy" Hauptmann (née Krause) joined us. Mother had gone to stay at the home of her private midwife for the birth. My first memory of meeting our new baby was when Father and I arrived to visit – Father opened the door to Mother's room and just at that moment the midwife was holding the new arrival up in the air by her ankles! I was so amazed and full of instant love and wonder. Mother stayed for approximately two weeks at this home following her confinement and during this period I spent all my time with Father, who was by now in charge of the police hospital in Graz. Every day, after school, I would meet Father and we would have lunch together before visiting Mother and our new baby in the evenings. Eventually the wonderful day arrived when we welcomed them both home and we settled into our new and happy family life.

Except, how could our lives *not* be touched by external events beyond our control? By summer things were changing more rapidly. In August Father told us the awful news that he was to be sent to Poland in November as part of the police detachment requisitioned by the Nazis to impose law and order in this country that Germany had invaded and taken by force. This was devastating news for us all, but for Mother particularly. I am sure she felt acutely aware of how his absence would affect our family and in some strange way she perhaps had a premonition of what life would be like without him and how the full responsibility for caring for their two daughters would fall heavily on her shoulders.

In September the news came that England had declared war on Germany, and we became even more aware of just how far this European conflict was to spread. The news was full of further Nazi oppression and dominance. We in Austria had had no option but to accept their power and, although we felt impotent and defeated, we certainly had no intention of welcoming this new regime. Quietly we tried to continue with our ordinary lives, anxious not to draw attention in any way but full of apprehension about the future.

November arrived and Father was due to leave us to take up his new role in Poland. During the First World War Father had been a medic and as a result of his previous training and experience he had been given responsibility for the Police Hospital in Graz where he was currently working. This hospital provided care for the police force and their families. As it happened, he was feeling rather unwell and, as he was certain that there was nothing seriously wrong with him, he 'self-medicated' rather than seeking advice from a doctor. In any case, he was unfit to be posted to Poland, much to our relief, but naturally we were concerned that he continued to be unwell. We spent our usual happy Christmas together – my baby sister's first encounter with the bright lights and magic of this wonderful occasion. However, on Boxing Day morning I was out walking with Father when I noticed him coughing up blood into his handkerchief. When we arrived home, I told Mother who called the doctor immediately and Father was admitted to hospital straight away.

Sadly, my beloved father died just four weeks later, in January 1940, of lung disease – the doctor referred to it as 'burning of the lungs'. Our lives were torn apart by his loss and Mother, especially, was totally grief-stricken, resulting in a complete nervous breakdown. She was admitted to a convalescent home in the country for two weeks where she had a chance to regain some strength and come to terms with the shocking and unexpected death of her husband. How was she to face this uncertain world and care for two children without him? The burden she carried was enormous. Meanwhile, I was left to care for my little sister alone for several days until a distant 17-year-old cousin came to stay and help. I was not quite 11 and my sister was 10 months old.

Shortly before my father died, he took my hand in his and looked straight into my eyes. 'Promise me, Herti,' he said, 'that you will always take care of your mother and sister.' I willingly took on this responsibility and from that day on I felt it my duty to ensure their safety. I had no idea what challenges I would face or how I would be required to fulfil this role but I am sure that my father's final request gave me the strength to withstand the adversity of the coming years, as well as a sense of purpose throughout my entire life.

Chapter 4

Dangerous Times

As Herti and her mother began the process of rebuilding their shattered lives, they did so to the backdrop of the ever-advancing Nazi war machine and its inexorable path towards war. Hitler was now the 'bully boy' of Europe, emboldened by the fact that Britain, France and America were reluctant to intervene in what were Hitler's precursory actions to full-scale war.

Hitler's ultimate desire in the war he was hell-bent on igniting was living space, or *Lebensraum*, in the eastern territories. To this end Hitler was to use Poland as the stepping stone. Plans to invade Poland had been implemented on 3 April 1939 when Hitler consulted his generals who began to outline the plan called Fall Weiss, which was the codename for the invasion of Poland. It set forth a proposal for the attack on Poland to begin on 25 August. The non-aggression pact which Germany had signed with Poland on 26 January 1934 and which set forth an agreement that both Germany and Poland should discuss any future issues via peaceful bilateral negotiation was a cruel deception. It was a deception that Nazi Germany would use on more than one occasion. Germany had no such intention of adhering to any of its peace agreements with its neighbours. Even the mighty Soviet Union had been cowed into a similar non-aggression pact with Germany, despite the fact that Hitler's *Mein Kampf* made it perfectly clear that an ideological war between Germany and the peoples of the east would be an inevitable course of action in the future. The peace that Adolf Hitler was proposing was merely a ruse for time – it was not worth the paper it was written on.

Herti would not be the only young girl whose life would be blighted by Germany's desire for war and conquest. Hilde Schubert, who had been born and raised in Vienna, came from a long military background: her grandfathers and great-grandfathers had all been men with strong military connections and her beloved father Alfred followed suit. Hilde recalls:

I was very young in 1939, just a 9-year-old, yet I have vivid memories of those times and how they affected our family. Ours was a large family comprising six children including myself. There was me, three older sisters and two younger brothers. My father, Alfred Franz Gotte, was a very strict yet very loving father. He always showed all of us great love and affection and each one of us adored him greatly. I can just about recall the little things that happened after the Germans invaded our country. There were many Germans in Austria and many felt that the union with Germany would be a good thing. My father was already a serving soldier in the Austrian army prior to the German takeover. After the Germans came, they gave him an ultimatum: he could either join the Wehrmacht or leave the service. I know this from what my dear mother told me in later years. My father had been with the Austrian artillery, he loved being a soldier and of course the Germans were keen to exploit his knowledge. He came home the one day wearing a completely different style of military uniform. The old Austrian army uniform was – how can I describe it? – it was more formal or traditional in appearance. Under the Wehrmacht he came home wearing a uniform bearing eagles and that dreadful swastika emblem. It had the appearance of something that signified an evil regime. I don't know, there was just something about it that told you this represented evil. Father had no choice in this matter, and he joined a Wehrmacht artillery unit. However, no sooner had he received a new uniform, identity document and other equipment than he left to begin training, no longer as an Austrian soldier but a German one. My mother was not happy about it at all, but the reality was neither Mother,

Father or us children had a choice in anything anymore. The training my father had gone for soon became clear to us. At the time he said nothing about it. He had probably been told not to talk about it, I am not sure. I remember him spending time away then returning home to us for a short period of time before leaving us again around late August of 1939. After that we waited for him as we thought he would come back in a week or so as he had done before. Then news began to filter in through the early morning on 1 September 1939 that German forces had invaded Poland. I recall my mother sitting by the radio which we had in our living room listening to the latest reports. The Nazi propaganda was spewing all this rubbish that the Poles had attacked the Germans first, forcing the Germans to retaliate. It was all lies, my mother told me all about it when I was a little older and able to fully grasp it all. I knew that my father was involved to some degree in this war Germany was waging. My eldest sister Katrin reassured me that Father, being in the artillery, would be far behind the front lines of the fighting, providing fire support for the forward troops, and that he would be alright. Katrin was not only the eldest of the six of us but the prettiest one too. I always thought how pretty she was and longed to be as pretty as she was. Katrin was our support along with Mother of course during these times of war. All we wanted to know was when our father was coming home and if this Hitler had now got what he wanted. We just wanted to get back to our normal lives, yet life was going to be anything but normal over the years that were to follow.

In a period of just thirty-five days the Germans crushed Poland. Poland fell to the death knell of the new German Blitzkrieg concept of an air force and army working closely together to rapidly overwhelm and destroy an enemy. The scream of Stukas filled the skies above Polish territory as the German ground forces advanced. The Poles did not go into the night quietly and fought with immense bravery though they were massively outnumbered and outgunned by their German enemy. By 6 October the invasion was complete and Poland was no longer a free, independent state. Russia had also assisted with the invasion of Poland, sharing in the spoils of a nation's downfall. It is strangely ironic that when Britain and France declared war on Germany over this invasion, they did not declare war against Russia who were clearly in alliance with Nazi Germany. It was yet another reflection of the cowardice displayed by the nations who had the opportunity and, arguably, should have intervened to prevent German aggression from gaining its foothold in Europe. By this time, it was too late: as those who had so willingly appeased Hitler now sat 'babbling' amongst themselves and preparing their declaration-of-war speeches, Hitler began to turn his attentions to the west with France and the Low Countries.

Hilde Schubert continues:

At home we continued to listen to the radio broadcasts which were just lies and propaganda. With a radio all you can do is just sit and listen to it. You don't see what the events being spoken about are like. You don't see people being killed or blown to pieces – the radio broadcasts simply gave people the news with that 'separation' in between, without blood being spattered all over people's faces: they could rejoice in the death of others without ever having to stare into the eyes of dead people. I began to loathe these broadcasts and the robotic German voice that came out from the radio. As I grew older, I left the room whenever these broadcasts came on. Our father returned home in the November of 1939 and we were happy that he was back with us for the time being. We thought that maybe now he could stay here with us in Vienna. Naturally, we asked our father about Poland, but he talked little about it – it was as if he was trying to distance himself from it all. I could see he was not happy about having taken part in it. I do recall him saying one time after he had drunk a little too much brandy one evening with some of our relatives: 'Proud, how can one possibly have any sense of pride in shelling civilians? That's what we had to do in Poland.' I remember an icy silence for some minutes before my sister Katrin skilfully broke the silence by playing a song on our piano to distract everyone. Katrin noticed as much as I had how Father's moods were slowly shifting. He drank more than he had ever done previously. I had rarely seen my father drunk. After Poland I would often come home from school to find Father slumped in his chair completely inebriated. Christmas of 1939 was a very good one for us, but I could tell Mother was tense not knowing if Father would drink too much and cause a scene. Thankfully the celebrations passed without any incident. We enjoyed the New Year celebrations and prayed like many others that 1940 would see an end to the war and violence blighting our nation. After Christmas Father went back to his unit for further training and this carried on right the way through the spring of that year, 1940. It was a relief to experience the springtime and gradually warming weather and, with the arrival of early summer, there was a lot of military activity. I saw a lot of aircraft, German aircraft, in the skies all heading in a westerly direction. As young people we would often be out playing with our friends and see convoys of trucks and tanks all moving west and hundreds of aircraft flying overhead. We would stop and watch them wondering where they were all going. Father had left us again in the April of 1940 and he told us he would write to us as soon as he knew anything. We knew something was going on with all of the activity of planes and things. There were unconfirmed rumours that Germany was about to attack the French and their British allies and that all of the activity was that of a 'giant' steeling itself to attack. Yes, we knew that the French and British had declared war on Germany but at that time it was as though no war was happening. We were not being attacked or bombed like we were in the latter years of the war. Our concern at that time was for our father: we understood that in war a soldier's luck can soon run out as a soldier lives his life from minute to minute, hour to hour, day to day. We just wanted Father back home and for the periods of long separation to end. It's not easy when you lie in your bed at night and all you can hear is your dear mother crying herself to sleep. It was incredibly hard for her and she tried to put on a brave face as they say, but you can only do that for so long.

Having conquered Poland, Hitler now turned his attentions to his enemies in the west. He was determined that the French would pay dearly for their part in Germany's humiliation of 1918, particularly the surrender and resulting Treaty of Versailles. The Nazi plan for the Blitzkrieg attack on France was a very simple one. The German forces planned to attack France from the most unlikely angle of the Ardennes Forest region of Belgium. Nobody expected the Germans to drive their tanks and artillery through the heavily wooded Ardennes and it was this feature of the Nazi planning which gave them the greatest element of surprise. The German military planners ascertained that by pushing through the Ardennes, and then the Somme Valley, they could cut off and surround the Allied units that had advanced into Belgium in anticipation of the German threat. The German forces were well organized and prepared and also possessing the essential element of air superiority over the battlefront. When the British and French forces met the German invasion, it was described by one British soldier as 'like being hit on the head with a sledgehammer'. Lance-Sergeant Erich Child who fought with the British Expeditionary Force (BEF) in France during May and June 1940 recalled:

We had been a little naïve in our military thinking and planning. When we came up against the first German assault it threw all our planning into chaos. At that time, we had no answer to the superior German tactics and firepower. Their planning had been far superior than ours had been: they had good armour at their disposal, the German troops were better motivated and disciplined and they had the element of air cover which we didn't. It sent us reeling – we had no answer to the German assault and were forced into a retreat. The discipline in some areas of the French army began to break down. Some of the French discarded their weapons and ran off. As we retreated, we were constantly harassed from the air by the Stukas [Junkers Ju 87 dive-bombers] which were relentless in their pursuit of our forces. Then there were the waves of German fighters. The Messerschmitts would target vehicles, anti-aircraft guns, artillery pieces and troop emplacements. They would come in at treetop height – you could see the spits of yellow flame coming from their wings as they fired their 20mm cannons. Their cannon fire tore up everything – you had to hide in a ditch or a hole until they had passed. We had to contend with this all the way to the little town of Dunkirk from where, after what felt an eternity, we were evacuated. How any of us escaped that hell I will never know. We were aware that the Germans had us completely at their mercy and that they had large numbers of tanks nearby that at any time could have been ordered to take the beaches of Dunkirk. It was very odd that they didn't attack when they had us trapped there. The main problem was the Stukas – there was not a Spitfire or Hurricane in sight. The only aircraft over Dunkirk at that point were German ones. Back home the Navy had requisitioned every conceivable kind of boat to be sent out to Dunkirk to rescue the BEF. All those ships and small boats that came out to rescue us were remarkable. If it were not for them, we would have had it – there would have been no more BEF! As we boarded our little rescue boat and began the trip back to England, I recall looking at the funnels of smoke coming up from Dunkirk and thinking about all those who hadn't made it this far. I lost a few good men along the way. At the time you don't think of them but suddenly here I was on my way home and they were lying dead somewhere back there. It didn't seem fair at all. I remember saying to myself as I looked back, 'That's it, France, you're on your own now. May God help you.' At the same time, I knew England would be next and the Germans would soon come. It was a very unnerving feeling back then.

As France fell the world again waited with bated breath in anticipation of Nazi Germany's next move.

Back in Austria in the town of Innsbruck lived Amelia 'Milly' Keller who was 8 years old in 1940. She was a pretty blonde-haired, blue-eyed girl often described as 'the girl with the golden smile'. Amelia, who was always known by her nickname Milly, had enjoyed a happy childhood with her mother and father, Celine and Gerhard Keller, until the Nazis took over their country. Milly also had a 6-year-old brother, Heinz, and older sister, aged 11, named Ursula. Milly recalls:

None of us could say we were happy that our country had been taken over by the Germans. We were even less happy about the things they were doing in our country. I remember first seeing them marching in perfect unison in their very smart uniforms. That's what I recall most, how very smart and disciplined they appeared. However, such looks were deceptive as they could be incredibly cruel and brutal. They made great efforts after the Anschluss to round up anyone of Jewish origin, political opponents and anyone they felt didn't fit into their 'little club'. I remember our old teacher had been found to have Jewish great-grandparents – she was a lovely woman and very kind, caring and intelligent. She disappeared a few weeks after the Anschluss and they replaced her with this 'ogre' named Gottfried Huhne. When I say he was an ogre he was just like the villain from some child's storybook. He was an imposing man with a cruel face and a cold persona to match. He personified the evil of the Hitler regime, had a neatly manicured Hitler-style moustache and it was blatantly clear that this man was a Nazi through and through. The morning he gave us his first class he had brought these large German flags with the swastika symbols on them. He had one either side of his desk and he had put a photo of Adolf Hitler up on the wall right in front of us so we could not miss it. He insisted, from that day on, when he entered the classroom that we should stand to attention and give a Hitler salute and a shout of 'Heil Hitler' whilst thrusting our right arm in the air in a salute. It was sudden and unwanted change for us and few of us liked it. My parents weren't happy about it, but what could they have done? This is what was so frustrating about it all; we couldn't do anything about it, or we were not allowed to speak out for fear of being investigated by the authorities. Huhne's style of teaching was as cruel as his facial features. He proclaimed that all the filth 'the Jew' had put into our brains would have to be removed. He told us that we, as Austrians, would one day thank the Germans for ridding our country of the Jews for us. Then he would talk about Hitler and his vision for a new Europe under German control. When we were asked the question, 'How many of you have read our Fuhrer's *Mein Kampf?*' no hands were raised in the class. Of course, this outraged him greatly that none of us girls had read this book. He then made sure every child's parent was made aware of its importance within the new educational ethos. He also made sure they understood that we were now effectively children of the Reich and obliged to adhere to the same rules as those children in Germany, that we as Austrians were no different anymore. My parents were horrified and very angry at the fact that they had to ensure I was schooled in the political 'filth' as they called it that was Hitler's *Mein Kampf*. I think they were worried it may somehow convert me to the Nazi way of thinking but even at 8 years old I knew what they were doing was morally wrong in every sense. My father sat with me as we went through the book and he wrote down key dates that he told me I should remember in case I was asked in class. These were things like Hitler's mother's and father's names and dates of birth, Hitler's date of birth, his political beliefs – oh God, the list was endless – but we had to learn it for our own good. I witnessed the violence that Huhne was capable of if one of us girls couldn't remember a question or give him an inappropriate answer. He once grabbed a girl by the back of her hair and, with his face twisted in rage, he shook her and ordered that by the next morning she should be able to give him a full explanation of what he wanted to know. I heard that the girl's father wanted to thrash Huhne but was prevented from doing so by the mother for fear of retribution. Our parents were powerless, and this man could do as he pleased with us. We were also obliged to join the Jungvolk movement, which was a Nazi movement for young children. The idea was to bring you under their control at the earliest age so they could then manipulate and exploit you to their own ends. It was a nightmare of militarism; our childhood was gone at this stage. We went out and played with friends after school and on weekends, but it wasn't the same anymore. I can remember after the fall of France and Dunkirk Huhne lecturing us on the current military territorial gains made by our victorious German armed forces. I recall one Saturday afternoon, several weeks after the British had left Dunkirk, a series of German trucks came through Innsbruck and some of them stopped. There were men in the backs of the trucks who jumped out to stretch their legs. They were guarded by German soldiers so had no way of escape. I had been playing with friends nearby and I watched the scene, fascinated by these rather scruffy-looking men. I knew from their uniforms that they weren't French and that they were British. They had very likely been captured in France or Dunkirk. I stood and watched them as they lit cigarettes and talked amongst themselves. I was always a very curious child and I wanted to go over to them, so I walked a little closer. One of the men said something to me but I couldn't understand English back then. He was unshaven and looked rather haggard, but he had a kind face and a kind smile, so I smiled back at him and said to him '*Halo*' which is 'Hello' in German. He obviously understood me as to my surprise he then said, '*Danke, danke*' (thanks, thanks). I smiled broadly at him again before one of the Germans guarding the men came over and told me in no uncertain terms, 'Bugger off, go away with you!' I looked at the German and I said to him, 'Sorry sir, I meant no harm. I was just watching.' I smiled at him and then he said to me, 'Alright, you can watch but you must keep your distance and you should not talk to these men.' I remember for the rest of that day I could think of nothing else but those poor British soldiers who were obviously on their way to one of the nearby prisoner-of-war camps. I later told my parents about what happened. They felt that same air of despondency but warned me to be careful and that I should not upset the Germans or 'break the rules' as they put it. I can also remember the Gestapo coming into our area and 'sniffing around' the houses where we lived. They were observing people to try and ascertain their allegiances. There was so much suspicion and throughout this time one had to just try and act normally and live a normal life. There were many in our community who were sympathetic to the Nazis and felt that it was right Austria should become a part of the Greater German Reich. As a young girl I never considered the dangers of challenging the Nazis or disobeying them. As a child you rarely sense the perception of danger that an adult might. It was a very dangerous time and you had to fit in even if you were not a Nazi. People disappeared without trace and no one dared ask where they went. My parents were forced into conforming in the same manner. My father did begin to receive better pay and quite a few perks under the new regime, but I think he and the other workers were just being seduced by the devil. However good it may all appear there was a price to pay later on.

Ellie Bergmann who lived in Vienna with her mother and father remembers how the dynamic of their lives altered once under the control of Adolf Hitler:

I remember my father's dilemma most of all. My father was a skilled blacksmith and was used to shoeing horses and repairing cartwheels and things like that. When the Germans came, they told him his skills would be better suited working for the Wehrmacht. At that time horses were used by the Germans in huge numbers and they needed men with skills like those my father possessed, so they drafted him. He didn't really have any choice. All men who were not too old and were physically fit were called up either for soldiering duties or security in the rear areas. I remember Father going away with many other men of our community for what would be their military training. My father had to learn to use a rifle, to march and things like that. After his training he arrived back home wearing the uniform of the German Army or Wehrmacht. It felt wrong to me, even as a child, that my father was going to be taken away from me and my mother just because this Hitler wanted to invade the rest of Europe. I secretly loathed the man, yet I was not alone in my feelings – many people felt the same way as I did. There was this silent hatred of Adolf Hitler yet everywhere you went you saw his face on posters. At school his portrait hung in the classroom – you couldn't get away from that cruel face of stone as I called it. Then there were the German soldiers within our community. They would walk around as if they owned the place. A friend of mine, a girl the same age as me named Hedrun, once stole a camera belonging to one of the German soldiers. He had left it with a pair of leather gloves on a table outside one of the cafés in Vienna. He left the table to go to the toilet or whatever and my friend grabbed the camera and the gloves and we both scurried off up a side street. She smashed the camera against a wall several times until she was happy it would no longer work and then she threw the gloves down a storm drain. I couldn't believe it, and I said to her, 'In God's name, don't ever get caught doing something like this or tell anyone as they will kill you for sure.' I never dared tell my mother and I only told her things like this long after the war had ended. There was another time when we were just out playing a game of skipping with a rope. Two smartly dressed Germans, who I think were in the air force [Luftwaffe], came strolling along. They congratulated us on our skills with the rope and told us their daughters back home in Leipzig played the same game that we were playing. Then they asked if they could take a photo of us to which Hedrun bluntly replied, 'No, sorry you can't!' She took me by the arm and literally dragged me away with her. I looked back at the two Germans who were just standing with bemused expressions on their faces; one just shrugged his shoulders and walked on. They didn't seem to understand that we simply didn't want to associate with them. Yes, we spoke the same language, but we were Austrians not Germans and were very proud of that. So, while our normal family lives had been disrupted by the Germans, we did carry on as best as we could despite them taking over and imposing their laws and rules on us. I would spend time with my grandparents too, usually on Sunday mornings. They were not happy about the Germans being in Austria either and were angry that they had drafted Father into the Wehrmacht. I knew my grandfather was deeply concerned about what was going to happen next. To lighten his mood, he often took me for a drive in his car in the summertime. We would just drive around the country lanes mostly but on one occasion he pulled over and he said to me, 'Here, get in the driver's seat. I am going to show you how to drive.' I sat there looking at him until he said again, 'Well, go on then – get into the driver's seat!' So, he got out of his seat on the left-hand side of the car and I jumped across into the driver's seat and took the wheel in my hands. I could hardly see over the top of it to see where I was going! Grandfather operated the foot pedals and gearstick while I just steered the car. It was great fun though not as easy as it looked. We slowly drove along a long lane flanked by tall pine trees with me steering the car until grandfather said, 'Well, that's enough for today but when you are older, I will teach you how to drive this thing properly.' From that day onwards when we went out for our little drives grandfather would always let me have a go. I guess it took both our minds off all the horrible things that were going on around us – disturbing events that we witnessed often. For instance, we saw the Jewish members of our community being made to clean dog excrement off the pavements and such like. All the time they were being goaded and ridiculed by the German soldiers and those stupid people we knew who supported what was going on in our country. Yes, there were a lot of people who felt the German presence in Austria was a good idea. This is why you kept your thoughts on the Germans to yourself. You couldn't trust anyone for there were always those who would betray you in an instant. I heard of people being found out for saying the wrong things about Hitler and other Nazi politicians. Sometimes they would just be beaten up; other times taken away for questioning. Some did not come back from the questioning. It was pretty obvious what had happened to these people.

Chapter 5

A Bloody Nose

With Poland and France defeated and a good proportion of the British Expeditionary Force miraculously rescued from the beaches of Dunkirk, there was an eerie calm about the world which waited in anticipation of Hitler's next move. The might of the German war machine was now staring across the English Channel. Hitler knew that in order to execute a successful seaborne invasion of England he would need total air superiority. Hermann Göring, chief of the Luftwaffe, assured Hitler in a proud boast that he could achieve air superiority within a few weeks, clearing the way for an invasion under the codename Operation Sea Lion or *Unternehmen Seelowe* in German. With the impending threat of a Nazi invasion Hitler had hoped that the British would sue for peace. Invasion was viewed only as a last resort if a peace agreement failed to materialize. Hitler had underestimated British resolve and it was made clear that the British were not prepared to negotiate any such peace terms with Nazi Germany. Meanwhile, German invasion barges began to assemble at various points along the French coast including Cherbourg, Le Havre, Boulogne, Calais, Dunkirk and Ostend along the Belgian coast. The Nazi invasion plan proposed five landing points on the British coast: these were Lyme Regis, Ventnor, Brighton, Dover and Ramsgate. Before any seaborne invasion of the British coast could be made even barely feasible, there were certain conditions that would need to be met. Firstly, there was the imperative that the Luftwaffe gain total air supremacy over the south of England. Secondly, the English Channel would need to be cleared of all British-placed sea mines situated around the various invasion crossing points, and the

Strait of Dover would need to be mined with German explosives at either end to deter any intervention by the Royal Navy. The third point of consideration was that the coastal regions between Nazi-controlled France and England needed to be reinforced with heavy long-range artillery pieces. Fourthly, and perhaps the greatest headache for the German planners of Operation Sea Lion, was the fact that the Royal Navy was still at large and would prove a significant threat to any invasion operation. It would have to be eliminated if any invasion across the English Channel were to have any hope of success. The German Kriegsmarine would have to be able to engage the Royal Navy in the North Sea to such an extent as to prevent its intervention in the German invasion crossing.

Ultimately, the responsibility of securing the conditions for a successful invasion of the south coast of England fell to the Kriegsmarine's Admiral Raeder and the Luftwaffe's Hermann Göring. Both men were open in their opposition to the German invasion plan, and both saw the many flaws in it. Raeder argued that the German Navy could not possibly achieve the objectives of the plan. The onus lay in the Luftwaffe's ability to destroy Britain's Royal Air Force (RAF) on the ground and in the air. Hitler proposed that the air attack phase begin in the early August of 1940. Should the Luftwaffe achieve its objective of securing air superiority, Hitler proposed that the invasion should commence around 25 August 1940. Britain indeed stood alone at that time, pondering the storm that was to come. As the British people mobilized in the face of Nazi invasion from across the English Channel, a 'giant was stirring' as Karl Voght recalled:

I was the pilot of a Junkers 87, a two-seater dive-bomber aircraft with a single engine fitted. I recall the first briefings for our aerial attack on the British. We were assigned various targets along the British coast, these targets including any shipping that we might encounter too. These first operations were fairly straightforward affairs: we would take off with an escort of Bf 109 fighters and head off towards Dover looking out for any shipping that might be in the Channel waters. There were always some ships in the Channel – most were relatively small but still targets of value carrying supplies to the British. As the Bf 109s ranged ahead looking out for any defending fighters, the only thing we had to be aware of was flak, or anti-aircraft fire, from the ships or nearby coastal positions. In fact, some of our aircraft attacked the anti-aircraft guns while others took on the shipping. The Stuka itself was a very accurate weapons platform, yet to hit a moving ship was no easy task at all. Sometimes it would take three Stukas to get one hit on a ship. We would climb to height above the target then peel off and dive down directly above it. This required nerves of steel as you were diving down at very high speed and there was no room for error. The bomb would be slung down on a special bracket: there was a viewing window in the cockpit floor so you could see the alignment of the bomb with the intended target. You released your bomb then the aircraft automatically pulled you out of the extreme dive. It was quite possible for both pilot and his rear gunner who sat at the back of the aircraft to black out under the immense G-forces. Usually it was the gunner who would see first if you had hit the target or not. Most of our bombs fell into the sea nearby. As all this was going on you would see an occasional Bf 109 falling from the sky trailing smoke where it had been hit by fire from enemy forces on the coast or by defending RAF fighters. The minute we released our bombs we headed straight back for home as fast as we could go.

The attacks against the RAF began on 10 July 1940 in a period which became known as the Battle of Britain. The British were not entirely at the mercy of the Luftwaffe and had the trump card of its defence strategy in the form of the Chain Home (CH) radar network along the south and east coasts. This invaluable radar network gave the defending British warning of any incoming Luftwaffe raid including their strength, height, direction and speed. These worked alongside the men of the Royal Observer Corps and were to prove decisive in defeating the Luftwaffe during the Battle of Britain. It is certainly true that the British came painfully close to defeat, yet, with no disrespect intended, it was neither the Spitfire nor Hurricane of the RAF that defeated the Luftwaffe. Whilst both the Spitfire and Hurricane were contributory factors to the German defeat, it was Hitler's intervention and insisting upon changing tactics and attacking London and other British cities, as opposed to continuing the focus of Luftwaffe attacks on the RAF and its airfields which culminated in the German defeat in the air war over England in 1940. Due to Hitler's interference the whole initiative was lost and would never be regained. I remember attending a seminar by former German Luftwaffe fighter pilot Adolf Galland who had fought against the RAF in the Battle of Britain and he recalled:

The interference in our tactical matters by both Göring and Hitler led to the Jagdgeschwader or Luftwaffe fighter wings becoming an ineffectual force in the battle. The job of the fighters was to fly ahead of the bombers, make contact with defending enemy fighters and inflict losses upon them. That way we were fighting a fluid campaign which suited our aircraft, the Messerschmitt Bf 109E, which we were using at the time. Our bombers were of course suffering heavy losses which were to be expected under the circumstances. Göring then insisted, after having arguments with Hitler, that the fighters had to stay close to the bombers: we could not range ahead and attack the RAF from higher altitudes which would have suited our tactics. By having to remain with the bombers we had to fly at slower speeds, thus using more fuel which gave us less time over the combat area and we were unable to protect our bombers as effectively. We also became as vulnerable as the bombers to the attacking RAF as we were stuck with the bombers like sitting ducks waiting to be attacked. This cost us many good pilots and aircraft. We could replace aircraft easily enough but not good pilots. At that phase of the battle we had no chance of winning – it was lost. Göring was frequently told of our complaints about these new tactics, yet he wouldn't listen, and he began to blame us for the heavy losses. This was immensely disrespectful, and I let my feelings be known to him and he didn't like it at all. Yet that was his problem – he refused to listen to us, the men who knew better than he did. From 7 September 1940 the focus of the air campaign was switched. The bombers were to attack London and other cities. This was in response to the accidental bombing of London by a disorientated Luftwaffe bomber crew resulting in the British retaliating by bombing Berlin, which infuriated Hitler greatly. Hitler then demanded that the focus switch to attacking British cities and so the Blitz began. The Battle of Britain was lost, and we had failed to gain the objective of air superiority although we came very close. Operation Sea Lion was postponed indefinitely, and we suffered our first real defeat at that stage. It was not a good feeling at all. People often ask, 'How did you lose when you were around two to three weeks or so from the collapse of the RAF?' I tell them, 'Our leadership lost its nerve at the crucial moment; they were adjusting military tactics to their emotional moods and they failed to listen.' We also failed to grasp the importance of the British radar network. I upset Göring once when, after shouting at us and blaming us for everything that had gone wrong, he looked at me and said, 'Look, what can I get for you?' So, I told him, 'A squadron of Spitfires.' He didn't like that, and he stormed off!

The much-vaunted Ju 87 Stuka dive-bomber which had proved so devastatingly effective in the Luftwaffe's conquest of Poland and France proved a total failure in the air campaign against the British. Stuka squadrons suffered such huge losses that they had to be withdrawn from the campaign. Stuka pilot Karl Voght explains:

The Stuka was not suited to operating in any theatre of war where our fighter groups did not have control of the skies. The Ju 87 was a tactical weapon devised to be used in conjunction with rapidly moving ground forces and where control of the air over the battlefront was in our hands. In the Battle of Britain, the Stuka Geschwaders only had minimal protection from enemy fighter attack. Our Bf 109s had such a limited period of combat time over the south of England, sometimes less than fifteen minutes, that they then had to turn for home leaving us at the mercy of the enemy fighters. The Stuka was not a manoeuvrable aircraft at all, and it was not fast: in fact, in the situation we found ourselves in over the south of England we were incredibly vulnerable and thus suffered heavy losses in the battle.

On 18 August I/Stukageschwader 77 lost ten of its aircraft while II/Stukageschwader 77 lost three and III/ Stukageschwader 77 fared little better losing two. Altogether, Stukageschwader 77's casualties on that ominous day amounted to a total of twenty-six men killed, six captured and six wounded. Voght concurs:

It was a disaster for our Stuka units. The 18th of August was one day I will always remember. That day we suffered badly in the air battle. I lost my gunner who sat in the back of the aircraft defending against attack from astern. It was hopeless, we were attacked multiple times. I did my best to avoid being hit but my gunner was killed when bullets came through the rear of the aircraft. He received wounds to the head and chest, any of which would have proven fatal. I managed to get our Junkers back home, but all the time I was flying back with a dead comrade in the back of the aircraft. The surviving crews landed back at the airfields exhausted and beaten having seen many comrades fall. An order came through shortly after the end of operations stating that we were to be withdrawn from the Channel battle for its duration.

In all honesty, I don't believe a seaborne invasion could have worked anyway, not without us suffering catastrophic casualties. The British Royal Navy was a powerful force and at the time we could not have competently dealt with them. I am sure it would have failed.

Back in Austria children such as Milly Keller were unaware that the Nazis had suffered their first bloody nose in their ambitions for world conquest. She recalls:

If you had a radio set, which we did, you could – if you dared – tune in and listen to the British BBC's World Service programmes. Our family were too afraid to risk doing this for fear of discovery. We heard rumours that the Gestapo could detect families attempting to listen to what they called 'enemy propaganda' and if anyone was found to be listening to this, they faced severe punishments as traitors to the Reich. So, we didn't dare do it; it was just too risky. Our mother and father were too concerned for our safety which was always foremost in their minds. In school no one ever mentioned anything about the German losses against the English, they just told you lies all the time and filled you with their propaganda. They would say, 'Our forces are engaged in a battle with the English and we shall be victorious; a German victory is assured, and our Fuhrer shall prevail.' This is the kind of rubbish they would tell us as children. Many of the adults were just as ignorant about what was really happening. My mother and father knew little other than what was printed in the newspapers which of course was all lies anyway.

Hilde Schubert had a slightly different perspective on how the war was going, as her father was serving in a German artillery regiment at the time. After the fall of France many German soldiers were able to enjoy something of a holiday and go out on sightseeing tours around the country. Hilde recalls:

My father wrote us letters and in some of the letters he would enclose photographs as proof that he was well and unhurt after the fighting in France. He wrote in one letter that he had been to Paris and seen the Eiffel Tower, one of France's greatest landmarks. He sent us a picture of himself with comrades with the tower clearly visible in the background. My father came home some weeks afterwards for a period of leave to be with his family. During this early war period it was felt best, if soldiers were not required for any immediate action or guard duties etc, that they should come home. When Father returned home, we thought he actually looked very well. He wasn't skinny and he had a nice suntan. He told us all about the invasion of France and how aircraft and artillery had paved the way for the German invasion of the country. He wasn't happy or jubilant about it though – quite the opposite. He told Mother the whole experience had made him feel like a criminal. He told us how the German forces had gone in and straightaway began rounding up any Jewish families there. He also mentioned that despite an unequivocal German victory, a resistance had begun almost as soon as the invasion had finished. My father had mentioned that he was told not to go out anywhere in France alone, that he should only do so as part of a large group and that they should carry their weapons with them at all times. The French may well have 'rolled over' quickly, but their country was pretty vast, and their resistance would continue fighting the German forces from within. The Germans brought in the Gestapo and the SS and had security divisions to combat partisans and resistance fighters. The Germans were afraid of resistance gaining any momentum and spreading back home. When people ask about resistance in Austria, I would say that yes, there was resistance but it was very slow in gaining any support as people were too afraid to join. However, with each year, resistance did grow as it does when any country falls under an occupation it did not ask for. For the time being we rejoiced in the fact that my father was back home with us. Though we knew at any time he could be called back.

As the bombing campaign by the Luftwaffe against England continued, Hitler considered his next move. His most ambitious plan of the war was that of invading the Soviet Union. The goal was to invade Russia which the Germans could then repopulate with German citizens for *Lebensraum* or living space for the Germanic peoples. In every sense the coming war with the Soviet Union was one based upon ideology. Despite the previous non-aggression pact that Hitler had signed with Soviet leader, Joseph Stalin, and their military co-operation during the Blitzkrieg against the Poles, Hitler despised the Slavic peoples of the east whom he termed as *Untermensch* – 'sub-human'. Stalin had been warned in advance of a possible German attack, yet had surmised that these warnings were nothing more than the result of western propaganda aimed at driving a wedge between the two military powers. It can be said that when the German invasion of the Soviet Union, Operation Barbarossa, began on 22 June 1941 it came as a rude awakening for the Russian dictator. For Germany, the ill-fated invasion of the Soviet Union would prove the ultimate 'nail in the coffin' for Hitler's Third Reich. Germany had neither the manpower nor resources to become bogged down in a protracted war with the mighty Soviet Union. Worse still for the Germans they now had a war which would have to be fought on two fronts, without doubt any military planner's worst nightmare, and in Germany's case it would be one which would come back to haunt its military forces time and again. The fighting in the east would come to epitomize not only Nazi barbarity but that of the Soviets too. Hitler's ideological battle would culminate in the deaths of 27 million Soviet people. Of this figure 8.7 million were military personnel while the remaining 19 million were civilians who died as a result of genocide, massacres, mass-bombing, disease and starvation.

* * *

Hilde Schubert's family enjoyed a brief period of happiness and normality before her father was again called up for military action. Hilde recalls:

My father was called up again, only this time it was clearly for something quite big. A few weeks before Father left some other men of his unit had called round to our house. One of the men was an officer. My mother and I were politely asked to leave the room while the men talked with my father. It was most unusual for my father to ask me to leave a room while he was in it. He had never done that before, and it all made me very suspicious yet inquisitive as to what was going on. I tried to listen at the door by placing my ear against it. I stood straining to hear every word until my mother came back downstairs and pulled me away from the door. This was not before I heard the word 'Russia' mentioned several times. When my father opened the door to the living room, I saw the other men rolling up documents which looked to me like maps. Was this some kind of unofficial military briefing? I asked myself. As the officer walked out, he stopped and looked down at me then asked, 'And what is your name, my young lady?' I replied, 'My name is Hilde, sir.' He smiled and patted my cheek before shaking my father's hand and walking out the front door. At dinner that evening I sat and toyed with my food until eventually Mother asked, 'Hilde, are you going to eat your food or just sit there playing with it?' It was at that point Father intervened and asked me, 'What is troubling you, princess?' He often called me his 'princess' when concerned about me. It was then I asked him, 'You will be leaving us again soon, won't you Father?' To which he replied, 'Yes, I may have to leave again soon, but I am a soldier and this happens when you are a soldier. Besides, it may not be for very long. It is not something for you to worry about. I need you and Katrin to be strong for your mother and younger siblings, so just think of them, okay?' At that I began eating my dinner and

Katrin, who was sitting opposite me, looked at me and flickered a smile, but we continued our meal in silence. A sense of foreboding permeated the air in our home. My younger sisters and brother seemed blissfully unaware of this shift in the atmosphere, which I felt at the time was perhaps not a bad thing – after all, isn't ignorance bliss, as they say today? The next day, before I went off to school with Katrin, an important communication arrived for my father. It was blunt in content and just an order that his unit was to return for duty with immediate effect. Katrin and I knew that by the time we returned home Father would be gone again. As I walked up the path with Katrin I stopped and looked back to where I could see Father running around like some headless chicken gathering his things with Mother in tow close behind him. I ran back and threw my arms around Father, who picked me up in his arms and spun me around and told me, 'Now, remember our conversation last night; don't worry yourself. I will return soon and in the meantime you and Katrin must look after your mother and the little ones.' Katrin then gave Father a big hug and he said the same to her, telling her not to worry about things. At that Katrin took my hand and we both walked to school. As we walked, we did so in relative silence, both absorbed in our own thoughts. Katrin held my hand very tightly. I looked up at her as she was so tall, at six foot a lot taller than me. I saw tears running down her face and so I stopped her and asked, 'Katrin, what is the matter? Why are you crying?' It was then she told me that Father was going off to war again, that she overheard him talking to Mother about some very big operation and that he would have no choice but to go. We never mentioned the word Russia. We had read much on European history and the wars that had torn it apart in the past. We had both read about Napoleon and his campaign in Russia, how it all went horribly wrong and ended in death and destruction. If that was where our father was going then we would rather not think about it. The subject was never discussed in our school until the actual invasion started and then there was talk about nothing else. On the blackboard the teacher scrawled with white chalk the word 'Untermensch'! She then went on to explain that the whole principle of invading Russia was to re-populate Russian territory with German people, to Aryanize the east which was at this time little more than a Bolshevik 'sewer' populated by the worst types of human breeding. She explained it as, 'Imagine you are moving into a grand old house. That house is hiding undesirable and unhealthy elements such as cockroaches, spiders and flies. Yet, it is otherwise a grand old house. What do you do? Naturally, the course of action you must take is to remove all of the pests and dirt which are attempting to cohabit alongside you.' That was her justification for the German invasion of Russia and removing the 'pests' as she so eloquently put it was through mass murder and genocide. Yet, when you are young you do not consider the underlying meaning of such words as 'remove'. The word 'remove' implies just that, doesn't it? It doesn't say force whole towns and villages to dig enormous pits then force them to stand in them before being machine-gunned to death. When the Nazis spoke of 'removing people' that is what they were doing. We knew this from little rumours that began to filter back from the fighting. There were wounded Austrian soldiers who had been sent to fight in the east under the Wehrmacht and they were appalled at what was going on there. We didn't hear much, but we heard enough to know that people were being rounded up and systematically killed as they were in all of the territories now under the new German Reich. In the east the Germans were carrying out a scorched-earth policy. They would wipe out whole towns and villages then burn them to the ground.

By the summer of 1942 Hilde's elder sister Katrin had left school and went to complete her compulsory *Landjahr* (year on the land) service. Hilde recalls:

It was very hard when Katrin left as it meant that I, as the eldest child at home, would have more responsibilities in helping Mother and my sisters and brother. I also had my schoolwork and the Hitler Youth for girls to focus on. When I joined the Jungmädelbund [Young Girls League] at the age of 10 I did so alongside many other local girls I knew. We all had the uniform too, which at first my mother was dead against. She didn't approve of any of us young girls wearing any uniform. It was the other local women who pressured her into buying me my uniform. It consisted of a brown-coloured jacket, white blouse, black tie and black skirt and a hat. My mother didn't buy the little jackboots, though, and I wore my own shoes when in uniform. The shoes were these brown leather sandal-type shoes which covered the toes but had an opening from the heel to halfway along your foot. These were ideal in summer as they kept your feet cool, but not very practical for the winter, even with thick socks on. The Jungmädelbund brought all the local girls together into a community where we did sports and learned Nazi teachings. The politics I had to absorb and understand, in case I was questioned upon it – which of course we were – but I knew it was evil and I knew it was wrong, along with the badges and uniforms we were wearing. I just did my best to please them and keep them happy, yet I didn't want to try too hard and become too proficient as they would single those types of girls out for what they called 'special duties' – which often meant being picked out as a potential JM leader or flag bearer or something like that. My aim was to do enough to keep them happy and keep them 'off my back'. I think secretly many of the other girls were thinking the same. I can recall at one meeting, this woman who we were told was someone 'big' or important visited. She spent ten minutes moaning at us, telling us we were not trying hard enough in our endeavours, that we were the worst group of Jungmädelbund girls in the area. I noticed some of the girls were trying hard not to laugh at her and

I myself was bursting inside, trying my hardest not to scream out with laughter at her. I think she was the wife of the local Nazi Gauleiter – I can't remember and, as I never saw her again, I quickly forgot about her and her sharp weasel-like features. So, I think many of us in that group were reluctant Hitler Youth girls, doing just enough to get by. You know, we were not as dumb as Hitler and his cohorts thought we were: we were far cleverer than we were ever given credit for.

Milly Keller was faced with little choice other than to conform as she, too, came of age in Nazi-occupied Austria. She recalls:

Joining the girls' Hitler Youth meant enrolling in the junior organization called the Jungmädelbund. It was compulsory so all parents had to enrol their children, but not before presenting their birth and ancestry records going back several generations to the local Hitler Youth authority in Innsbruck. The birth and ancestry records were scrutinized very thoroughly and, if they were satisfied there were no Jewish blood lines, the next stage was a medical and physical examination. I didn't like this part of it at all. I went for my examination with my mother and these people found me a fascinating specimen, I'm sure. Yes, I had the blonde hair, the blue eyes – oh, they did rejoice in my Aryan qualities! They looked at my hair, eyes, teeth, ears, legs, feet then measured my head and height. I felt like some cow at a market being selected before being auctioned off for the highest price. It was intrusive and more than a little humiliating. Girls like me were labelled as 'the special girls' of the Hitler Youth. They complimented me on my Aryan attributes and my natural beauty. At that time my thinking was, 'God, this is embarrassing!' and I just wanted it over so I could go back home with my mother. After my examination and subsequent 'pass' stating I was fit and healthy for the Jungmädelbund they had a short conversation with my mother in private. As we left the building, I asked my mother what they talked to her about, but she wouldn't say anything, just telling me, 'It was nothing.' However, it became obvious later that this was not entirely true. All the young girls in the Innsbruck Jungmädelbund with blonde hair, blue eyes and with pretty faces were set aside from those with dark hair and dark eyes. The Nazis wanted us as their 'poster girls'. We were often photographed for the Hitler Youth Year Books and for their propaganda. At any of the important Hitler Youth events we were encouraged to stand at the front of marches and carry flags and things. I didn't want to be in their spotlight, and I didn't want to be one of their 'special girls' and I didn't want to be an Aryan. I just wanted to be a normal girl, play with my friends and go to school but it was becoming clear they had other ideas for us. The Hitler Youth leaders talked persistently about our roles as future mothers and stressed that all other considerations should be secondary to this vital task. We visited maternity homes and hospitals where we were introduced to the rudiments of childcare for some first-hand experience. I recall the first time I ever held another woman's infant other than the ones from our own family. I held the little girl in my arms, and she gurgled happily and even smiled at me. As I held the baby girl, I couldn't help but feel a surge of emotion and sadness which came over me both at the same time. It was a strange feeling I couldn't identify. When I handed the baby girl back to her mother, I felt tears well up in my eyes. The other girls with me admitted to feeling the same emotions afterwards. Was this our maternal instinct being provoked as part of our 'special duty to the Reich'? It certainly occurred to me afterwards that this was the motive behind such visits. I had always wanted to work in clothes or fashion when I was older, maybe design my own clothes and sell them. The problem was the Hitler Youth had other ideas and plans for us which we were unable to deviate from. I wasn't happy with it all from the start but now I hated it all even more. As we had dinner one evening, I said to my mother, 'It's the Nazis' fault that Katrin has had to go away. It's their fault I have had to join their Nazi girls' league. I hate them.' My mother immediately retorted, 'You can't say those things! You must never speak those words again, Milly. If someone were to hear you and report you, we would all be in big trouble. You have to understand we must comply with the rules and the law.' I felt trapped, like we were all in some helpless situation. I knew then that our only salvation lay in the defeat of Hitler. When my father arrived home from his job on the local railway, he took me aside and gave me a lecture too. He told me in no uncertain terms that I was to keep my mouth shut, to never speak out against the authorities again as it was too dangerous. I think my father felt that the Nazis had done men like himself a huge favour. Father couldn't have served in the military due to a previous accident on the railway which had injured his left leg. His work was seen as a high-value profession and thus he was looked after well by the Nazi authorities. Of course, the railroad network at Innsbruck was instrumental in carrying various cargoes and supplies of raw materials towards Hitler's war effort. I hadn't thought of that initially and it soon occurred to me that we were 'stuck between a rock and a hard place', as they say.

What Milly Keller wasn't aware of at the time was the fact that the 'German Giant' had been dealt the first of many fatal blows. Britain had stood firm against what looked to have been overwhelming odds against her, and by doing so had dealt the German war machine its first 'bloody nose' of the Second World War. The myth of Nazi invincibility from this point onward would steadily diminish.

Chapter 6

Limbo

The loss of Herti's beloved father had a huge emotional impact upon her family which now included a newly born baby sister the family always called Mädy. With the support of family and friends Herti and her mother were able to move forward in an attempt to pick up the pieces of their lives, something Herti was determined to do, with her father's dying wish firmly in her mind. Back in those difficult times, to lose the head of the household would have been something of a disaster for most families. In many such cases mothers, often stricken with melancholy, found themselves unable to cope, forcing them to send their children to live with grandparents or other relatives. It is a reflection of both Herti and her mother's remarkable strength of character that the loss of a father and a husband did not destroy their once happy family. Herti recalls:

The next few months passed in a blur. Our life was in a kind of limbo as we adjusted to the shock and change. Somehow the loss of my father brought home to us the tragedy that was befalling so many families, only our loss was the result of sudden illness rather than the wilful destruction of some families' lives. The grief we felt was overwhelming and it took months before we felt some sort of equilibrium return and were able to face a new 'normality'. Our relatives rallied round and were as supportive as they could be, but ultimately Mother had to make a new life and gain the strength to manage everything on her own. After the two weeks she spent convalescing she returned home to pick up the pieces of our life and I was able to go back to school.

Once back at the grammar school in Graz, in which I had enrolled the previous September, my head teacher, Professor Margareta Heritsch, was extremely supportive and, indeed, the whole staff gave me great help over the next few years. As well as being head teacher, Professor Heritsch was also my English teacher – she had a sister, Gertrude, who had been the first woman to swim the English Channel! Gertrude lived in England and this connection had enabled Margareta to become very proficient in the English language. I feel certain that the help this woman gave me contributed significantly to my love of learning English – a skill that, sooner than I imagined, proved to be incredibly useful in the following years and that helped to shape my future life.

At home I enjoyed listening to the BBC World Service on the radio, even though it was strictly forbidden. In order to listen without anyone knowing I would only tune in during the evenings and would make sure the volume was on a very low setting. In hindsight, this activity was pretty risky – if I had been reported to the authorities there would have been severe consequences. However, I was prepared to take a chance and my English skills benefitted enormously whilst I also gained a wealth of knowledge about what was actually happening in the war, rather than being indoctrinated solely by Hitler's propaganda.

About this time Mother started taking in student lodgers to supplement her police widow's pension. The students were studying at the renowned and highly acclaimed Graz University. We would have one lodger at a time and there was a mix of male and female students who stayed with us. Since they lived in our house as a member of the family, we got to know them well and I enjoyed their company very much.

During this period of transition within our family many changes were taking place in school and also in the wider community. The impact of the Nazi forces affected our lives in ever-increasing ways. Firstly, at school all religious education was stopped. Whilst churchgoing was still acceptable, within school there was no longer an opportunity for us to be 'indoctrinated' with any ideology other than Nazism.

The indoctrination Herti mentions here would not only have occurred within her school education but within that of the Hitler Youth. Membership of the Hitler Youth was by this time compulsory and all the children of the Third Reich were expected to join their respective Hitler Youth organizations. Young girls from the ages of 10 to 14 were to enrol into the Jungmädelbund (JM) or Young Maidens League, while girls from 14 to 18 were to join the Bund Deutscher Mädel (BDM) or League of German Maidens which was the senior Hitler Youth organization for girls. A uniform which consisted of a brown jacket, dark skirt, white blouse and black tie and walking boots was available to those who could afford it. Those girls whose parents could not afford the uniform were permitted to wear clothes of their own choice. Sporting wear often consisted of a pair of black shorts and a white vest bearing the diamond-shaped Hitler Youth motif at its centre. Sporting footwear consisted of a pair of plimsolls, bare feet or the girls' own shoes. The activities of these two Hitler Youth organizations for the girls were twofold: twice a week, usually on a Wednesday evening and a Saturday afternoon, there would be meetings which every member was expected to attend. On the Wednesday evenings, subject to weather and regional variations, it was usually a mixture of political and racial theory, which would be discussed, along with readings from *Mein Kampf* and then physical exercise. The girls were required to have a sound knowledge of this 'devil's work' and were often asked to recall passages from the book from memory. If a girl could not give a satisfactory explanation, she could be subject to punishment. Saturday afternoons were a little more exciting as this was often the sports afternoon, concerned primarily with all manner of sporting events. Running, ball throwing, gymnastics, team events in which the girls made themselves into human pyramids, archery, javelin, shot put and long jump were just some of the disciplines. In the rural areas the curriculum differed slightly with more emphasis on traditional dancing. The two organizations also had their yearly summer camp where the girls were taken out into the forests and taught many useful skills such as orienteering, making fires and cooking. On these summer camps the girls had to erect tents to sleep in at night. They would all be under the watchful eye of a JM or BDM leader. First thing in the morning the girls would be roused for roll call and fitness exercises usually followed by swimming in one of the many lakes in the countryside. After these early morning activities, the girls would prepare breakfast, wash and dress and go out on a march where they would carry their banners and sing patriotic songs. Discipline was of paramount importance and no makeup, perfume or jewellery was permitted to be worn. For those girls who excelled in their Hitler Youth community a series of awards, badges and certificates could be earned. It would lead many girls to aspire to become JM or BDM group leaders themselves. These positions carried with them a huge amount of prestige within the Hitler Youth, but also led to a diminishing of parental control whilst furthering the Nazi influence. The girls were also schooled intensively in first aid, learning how to treat cuts, burns and broken bones – ironically all the kinds of things one might encounter in a wartime situation. It all appeared quite idyllic to many, yet there were sinister intentions with both these Hitler Youth organizations. By enrolling the girls into the Hitler Youth community, it was far easier to remove their parental authority and to influence individuals into the Nazi ethos and ways of thinking. The girls were primarily educated towards childbearing and domestic life, to marry, stay at home and look after a husband and have as many children as possible. Hitler was anxious to secure as many children as possible for the future Third Reich. He understood that territorial gain and control of the world as he viewed it could only be achieved through war. He would need a willing supply of young soldiers to replace those lost in the battles that lay ahead. The sad irony of all this was that many young girls would not realize that they were to become yet another resource to be exploited until it was too late. The girls under Adolf Hitler's Third Reich were to be his biological Nazis, skilfully influenced away from all professions other than those of child-bearers and homemakers. In order to instil this motherhood quality within the girls, many were placed in maternity homes where they helped mothers with their newborn babies. JM and BDM girls were also sent to kindergartens where they looked after young children. By the time they were 18 many girls were fully proficient with all aspects of childcare. The males were viewed as the masters of the Third Reich and, to this end, the boys had their own Hitler Youth organization which oriented them primarily towards being soldiers.

Herti was aware of the underlying evil of the Hitler Youth ideology, although she thoroughly enjoyed the physical activities and sports, recognizing that the benefit she received from the fitness training was to prove invaluable to her in the challenging situations she was to encounter in the years ahead. She recalls:

A huge emphasis was placed on physical education and fitness and we were all obliged to participate in regular sporting activities. Each morning, at the start of each school day, we would assemble in the school yard for a half-hour game of Volkerball (similar to volleyball). Afterwards the swastika flag would be hoisted, and all students had to stand to attention with their hands raised in the Nazi salute. Twice a week we had indoor athletics for an hour and every Wednesday and Saturday afternoon we had to report to the sports ground in Graz where we would take part in sprinting, relays, long jump and high jump for two hours.

All girls and boys between the ages of 11 and 14 were obliged to join the Hitler Youth. After the age of 14 the girls then became members of the BDM. My role as a member of Hitler Youth was as a flag bearer at any special occasion and I recall carrying this responsibility when Hitler himself visited Graz on an official engagement as well at numerous political rallies or events. I vividly recall the occasion when we all lined the streets, smartly dressed in our uniforms, as we awaited the arrival of the Fuhrer's motorcade. As his large, black, open-topped car drove slowly past, Hitler stood upright, scrutinizing the crowds with his arm raised in his infamous salute. His face was cruel and hard, emphasized by his clipped moustache and his fixed, stern expression. I remember feeling a sense of disgust at this 'horrible man', but what was I to do except obey my orders to raise and lower the swastika flag as I had been instructed? This was supposedly an honour, but I felt no sense of pride. None of these activities was in any way 'optional' – we were obliged to participate, and the consequences of refusal would have been unimaginable. I cannot stress too much how impotent and helpless we felt to object to any of the impositions the Nazis placed upon us. In addition, it was already becoming apparent that one could not know for sure where other people's sympathies lay, so it was essential to keep one's own counsel or risk being exposed. Trust and certainty were becoming rare commodities: the fear of betrayal was only too real.

By the age of 12 I had started skiing and at 13 I went on a mountain rescue course which would qualify me to participate in rescue operations to secure injured skiers from the mountains. There were six girls on my course, all from different parts of Austria. The course was extremely intensive and challenging, especially for such young girls staying away from home. We were often up until the early hours of the morning, going over the day's lessons and making sure we understood everything we had learned. Not only did we have to become proficient at First Aid, we also had to be competent and strong skiers so we could carry a stretcher while skiing to the bottom of the mountain. As it was wartime, for the duration of the course we had to wear white ski outfits in order to be camouflaged against the snow. At the end of four weeks we all passed our exams and enjoyed a party atmosphere with the people of the village before we returned home.

During the winter I also enjoyed skating and we were fortunate enough to have a lovely outdoor rink in the town. In the evenings it was particularly beautiful as the rink was lit up, the ice glistening and sparkling brilliantly. Experienced skaters had a special area where they could enhance their skills by dancing to music. How I enjoyed this magical place where, for a while, everything could feel free and exhilarating. I would be reminded of how I would dance to the music in the cafés with Father on Sunday mornings – yet again music would transport me, and I would transcend the trials that surrounded us.

I worked hard at all my lessons, determined to succeed academically and becoming ambitious to achieve the best possible grades, which I saw as a way to reward my mother for all her loving care and for my father – surely this was how I could ensure that I carry out his wish that I care for my mother and sister. My ambition was to go to university to study medicine. There were few things we had any choice over but working hard at school was one thing I could do to make sure I was equipped for the future, whatever it might hold.

During our holidays, we continued to visit Laxenburg and the bakery that still enthralled me with its mouth-watering, fabulous aromas of freshly baked cakes and bread. Even though my grandparents and father were no longer with us, this special place always rekindled memories of happy times before we lost our loved ones and our freedom. One summer's day, when I was 13, I was given the responsibility of taking Mädy and my cousin to the big park surrounding the Royal Palace where there was a boating lake. At the entrance to the park was a memorial statue. I remember there were very few people around that day, so my attention was drawn to a solitary figure – a man wearing a large overcoat. As we drew closer, this man turned towards us and suddenly opened his coat wide, revealing that he wore nothing beneath! Quickly I distracted the little children and we hurried away, proceeding into the park to enjoy our afternoon in a boat on the lake and a tasty picnic. Why I was not afraid we would be followed I have no idea – perhaps this was another example of how I was able to take such events in my stride. Nevertheless, I was shocked by this episode and when we arrived home, I told my mother and auntie what had occurred. They went swiftly to the police to report what had happened. I include this event because it is an occasion that I feel was an important learning experience for me – I was confronted by something frightening but was able to remain calm, look after the little children and act responsibly.

One of the striking differences between Laxenburg and Graz was that Laxenburg, being close to Vienna, had much more exposure to the Jewish population that was significantly greater in this area. Consequently, there was greater awareness of the eradication of the Jews in this region – people who had been accepted by all my family at the bakery as our friends and neighbours for as long as I could remember. Whilst there was little that could be done it was clear that the people of Laxenburg and Vienna were generally sympathetic to the plight of the Jews. However, in Graz things were different. There was not a large Jewish community so generally people were not constantly confronted by the removal of their neighbours. Many citizens did, in fact, sympathize with the Nazi regime so as time went by, more and more one did not know whom to trust.

So, by the time I was 14½ and was ready to start the autumn term of 1943, I was feeling fairly confident that I had already been able to overcome a number of challenges in my life. I was physically very fit, thanks to our regular PE regime, my time with Hitler Youth, skiing and skating. I was constantly improving my academic skills, in particular my English language abilities. I felt proud and confident that I was capable of looking after Mädy and of protecting her and I felt I was being a supportive daughter to Mother who was doing her very best to keep all of us safe. I was not afraid to carry on with my subversive and clandestine listening to the BBC and was determined to learn as much as possible about what was going on elsewhere. Though dominated and controlled by the Nazis we were in no way complicit with their ideology and, though no one would dare say it, we longed for the time when – however unlikely it seemed – Hitler's forces would fall.

Herti's longing for the ultimate failure of Nazi Germany – of which she was no willing supporter – was somewhat prophetic. By 1943 Hitler's fortunes in the east had shifted dramatically. The early success of Operation Barbarossa of 1941 was soon overshadowed by a series of military disasters for the German forces engaged in the fighting in the USSR. The Russian foe was proving to be a far more formidable adversary than the German forces had ever anticipated. The winter conditions in the east, which the German forces had been wholly unprepared for, had also proved an obstacle to the German war machine which in the extreme winter of 1941 ground to a halt in freezing temperatures which dropped to as low as –50°C. The German Army lacked the proper winter clothing and supplies and their weapons, vehicles and equipment began to falter under these dreadful conditions.

Ellie Bergmann recalls one of the many stories her father told her about the winter of 1941 in Russia:

My father said to me once that he was so lucky being in charge of caring for the horses. The horses were used to pull carts containing supplies and horses also pulled artillery guns. When the freezing Russian winter arrived, he told me that he would often lie down with the horses during the night as they were a great source of warmth. He told me how he watched men slowly die from the freezing weather. He also told me he saved the life of one young German corporal who was suffering badly from the cold by getting him to stand between the horses to keep warm. Father told me if it weren't for those horses, he probably would never have made it back home to us.

The logistical issues facing the Germans during the winter of 1941 were considerable. Hermann Göring gave Hitler his assurance that the Luftwaffe could maintain supplies to the troops despite the conditions, but such assurances were delusional, as Karl Voght recalls:

You couldn't take off in the kinds of conditions we were experiencing in the winter of 1941. If you were able to take off and you got caught in a blizzard your chances of getting back to your airfield were literally zero. It was impossible to fly aircraft in those conditions. The engines wouldn't start, the weapons would freeze up and not function and the crews would get severe frostbite. I remember one Junkers 88 taking off one morning in poor conditions. The crew were taking some Luftwaffe officer a short hop of around ten miles to a forward unit. We watched the crew and this officer climb aboard; the engines were fired up and it taxied out onto a runway of ice. We watched it take off and immediately vanish into the grey metallic gloom of the winter sky. That Junkers 88 was never seen or heard from again until, I think, it was found many years later almost intact where it had crash-landed. There were no signs of the crew, no letters, no bones, clothing, remains or anything else. It was very likely that they crash-landed and if any of the crew did survive, they may have been taken and killed by the Soviets or attacked and eaten by bears. That winter of 1941 was a curse – to try and explain how cold it was is impossible. We lost thousands of men to the weather – men whose eyelids turned black and dropped off, men who lost fingers and toes to frostbite. Some just got so cold they lay down and gave up and death claimed them soon after. I remember a sentry who had to be relieved on one occasion. The guy taking over from him walked up and tapped him on his shoulder and told him he could now go inside for a rest. There was no reply from the sentry – he had died and had frozen solid. It took several men to carry him away. He was like one big block of solid ice.

In 1943 the Germans had tasted defeat in the infamous Battle of Kursk widely recognized as the largest tank battle in history, the Battle of Belgorod, the Fourth Battle of Kharkov, the Battle of Smolensk, the Battle of the Dnieper, the Battle of Kiev and the Dnieper-Carpathian Offensive.

With America's entry into the Second World War, following the Japanese attack on Pearl Harbor in December 1941, Germany would soon find itself under attack from one of the greatest industrial powers in the world. Soon bomber aircraft of the mighty United States Eighth Army Air Force would join Britain's RAF in a sustained 'around the clock' bombing campaign against cities within the German Reich, Austria included. US bomber aircraft based largely in the East Anglia area of the UK were within easy reach of all the major German cities. The strategic bombing of Germany was viewed as an essential component in destroying not only Germany's infrastructure, factories and logistical centres but also the morale of its people.

It was agreed that while Britain's RAF would bomb territories in the Reich by night, the US Eighth Air Force would attack Germany in large-scale daylight raids. It was perfectly clear by this stage of the war that the defeat of Nazi Germany was now just a matter of time. Many battles, setbacks and difficult times still lay ahead, yet Allied commanders were now confident that the tide of war in Europe was turning in their favour.

* * *

Life for Milly Keller and her family in Innsbruck had been a relatively quiet affair up until the December of 1943. Milly recalls:

It was just ten days away from Christmas Day on 15 December which, I believe, was a Wednesday. It came as a complete shock, out of the blue, when forty-eight American B-17 bombers of the 301st Bombardment Group came over the city and dropped bombs on us for the first time. There had been no prior warning that I can recall and as a result some 259 people were killed, 500 were wounded by blast and shrapnel while 1,627 were made homeless in that first bombing raid. It was said that 126 tons of bombs had been dropped on Innsbruck in that first raid. We were lucky as our house had not been affected in this attack. There was, all of a sudden, considerable rage against the American forces. It was a sad fact that after that first raid the Nazis gained a lot of new supporters. I remember in the aftermath of the raid being in a state of panic over my father – was he alright or was he caught in the attack? It was a huge sense of relief when he returned home shortly after the raid. Father was very shocked and he looked pale and was shaking. The girls and boys of our Hitler Youth group were quickly mobilized to help those people who had been hurt, lost families or made homeless. This was my first glimpse of what war was really like. Up until this point I had never seen what bombs could do to a human body. Our group leader assembled us all and took us down to the affected areas of Innsbruck. As we passed by ruined buildings that were still burning away, we saw recovery teams pulling arms and legs out of the piles of rubble and throwing them into bathtubs. Bodies, if not blown apart, resembled ragdolls. It was a scene from hell and I felt a surge of nausea shoot through my body. The group leader noticed this and shouted, 'Girls, look to the front and keep going!' When we arrived in the city, we had to set up a kind of mobile kitchen where soup and bread would be provided to feed those made homeless. We were instructed to go around the crowd of people and offer consolation and warm words of reassurance. What good were warm words of reassurance to these poor people? I can remember thinking. I sat with a young woman and her two young sons. The woman was trying to comfort the two quivering little ones so I sat beside her and asked her if she needed any help and if I could get anything for her. She just looked at me and although she appeared to be still in shock herself, she gave me a faint smile and held my hand for a few minutes. Her hands felt so cold, so I began to rub them with mine to warm them up. I asked her if she needed me to inform any relatives or family for her and she reassured me that she would now be going to stay with a sister away from this place. I asked if she had a husband here and she told me he was in the army away fighting. I didn't feel it would be right to ask her too many questions, so I just sat with her and held her hands. When the food at the mobile kitchen was ready, I left the woman and her two boys to go and help distribute soup and bread rolls with the other Hitler Youths. I did go and take soup and bread to this woman and her two boys and I also took her a blanket and wrapped it over her and her two boys. The boys were stunned, pale and obviously suffering much fear. One kept staring up at the sky, his eyes wide with terror as if looking out in case any more planes came. I had to leave them as there were many others that needed our help. Before I left the woman, she asked me my name so I told her, 'My name is Amelia Keller, but you can call me Milly as everyone who knows me calls me Milly.' She looked up at me and said, 'Take care of yourself Milly, and if I never see you again, I would like to say thank you for your help.' At that I left her and carried on helping the others. By the end of the day I felt exhausted and by the time I got home I just wanted to go to bed and sleep. At the kitchen table our family had gathered, and we sat in silence as we ate a small meal of stew. We were thankful of still being alive and well, but we were all concerned at what would happen next? Would the bombers return? Would it be our turn next? As I lay in my bed, I closed my eyes and all I could see was the woman with the two little boys. I lay in bed and cried like a baby. My sleep that night was disturbed by the visions of corpses, fire and destruction. I awoke in the morning feeling like a zombie.

On Sunday 19 December a force of around a hundred B-17 bombers attacked the railway marshalling yards at Innsbruck. This second raid found the German military forces in a higher degree of preparation than the previous attack. Fighter aircraft of the Luftwaffe were airborne and ready to intercept the incoming force of Allied bomber aircraft. A huge aerial battle ensued over a large area of Tyrol and northern Italy. Initially, the American bomber force scored direct hits on the provincial capital's train station killing seventy people, and subsequently was diverted away to Schwaz, where their bombs caused relatively little damage. The civilian population again received little warning of this raid and few had taken to their air-raid shelters as a result. However, casualty figures for this raid were not as great as that of the earlier attack of 15 December. I was unable to find any reliable record on how many Allied bombers had been lost on this particular raid at the time of writing and time did not permit further research. What is known is the Allied bombing offensive against Innsbruck and other targets was suspended for some six months due to the preparations for Operation Overlord in Normandy, France. During this period of respite, the German military had time to reorganize its anti-aircraft defences in the area and greatly expanded its network of air-raid shelters in and around the city. These air-raid shelters were mainly constructed by forced labourers requisitioned from the Arbeitslager Reichenau – the Reichenau Labour Education Camp – in Innsbruck. By 1944 the network of underground air-raid shelters would provide safety for some 28,755 Austrian civilians. By the time the Allied bombers returned to attacking the railway marshalling yards at Innsbruck, they would find a mercilessly heavy, intense and accurate barrage of flak awaiting them.

Milly Keller recalls:

I remember seeing all these large guns being brought into the city. Most were towed in on the backs of lorries or other vehicles. I recognized some of these weapons as the formidable German 8.8cm Flak cannon. Some of the Flak guns were set up in the fields outside the city so a kind of ring of defences was created. There were also these anti-aircraft guns which had four barrels and fired rapidly: these were for low-flying targets. Many purpose-built air-raid shelters were constructed, and we even had one in our back garden. Ours was dug into the ground at the far end of the garden – we used wooden planks to form the roof and then placed soil on top of this. Whether or not it would prove effective we didn't know, but it was there if we needed it and would be safer than staying in the house if and when bombs fell around our area. All we could do at that time was pray that this would all be over soon. I wasn't so much angry with the Allied airmen; I was angry with the Germans who had brought this upon us in Austria. I remember one morning a German truck towing a gun pulled up close to our house. I watched as the driver and his comrade walked off down the road. When they had disappeared from sight I ran into our pantry and took my mother's remaining supply of sugar. I took the sugar and carrying it behind my back I walked over to the German truck, undid the fuel cap and poured the sugar into it. I just felt angry at them and wanted to vent my anger against them. I ran back into the house looking around and hoping no one had seen me. I went out into the back garden where my mother was doing some washing. She knew I had done something as I was breathing heavily and shaking from nerves. She always knew when we kids had done something and she stopped what she was doing, looked me straight in the eye and asked me, 'Milly, what have you been up to? You have guilt written all over your face.' I sat silently looking down for a moment before telling her I had poured her precious sugar supply into the petrol tank of the German truck which was parked outside our house. I knew the next ninety seconds were going to be bad as she remained still for a moment then grabbed me by my arms and shook me shouting, 'What on earth have you done that for? What if they come around the houses wanting to know who sabotaged their truck? Then what do we do? Do you realize how stupid you have been?' As Mother continued her tirade, she was stopped by the sound of a truck starting up out at the front of our house. We both rushed inside and peered from behind the curtains. The truck I had sabotaged had started up and was driving off down the road. I was grateful in a sense as there would have been big trouble. My mother was probably more relieved than I was. She threatened me to 'never, ever do anything like that again' and told me, 'If ever your father found out about this, he would go mad!' The funny thing was my father came back from work later in the afternoon and described how he had come across two irate German soldiers who were stranded with their truck and an artillery piece at the roadside around a mile away. One of them had his head under the bonnet saying it looked as if the fuel line was damaged or blocked, he wasn't sure. As Father recounted what he saw Mother was busy knitting, but she looked up at me and gently shook her head then smiled as she began knitting again. It was only months after the war had ended that I told my father that I had poured Mother's sugar supply into the petrol tank of that stranded German vehicle he came across. He grumbled about what a stupid and dangerous thing it was to do but had to admit that his 'golden girl Milly had some nerve'. As the bombing increased in its intensity, school was disrupted. It wasn't safe to go out as we used to. We came to dread the sound of the air-raid siren – it was a warning that death was on its way. I recall the boys in particular going out after the raids to look for bomb splinters and bullet casings. We girls often went with them as if you found something good you could then swap it for something better. I once found the nose cap from a shell and all the boys went mad over it offering me the few sweets they had and marbles and things. Of course, I gave the nose cap up straightway when offered sweets. They were nothing much – homemade boiled sweets using boiled water and some sugar, yet I liked them.

When the bombing of Innsbruck increased, the authorities wanted civilians to leave the city, particularly the industrial areas near the railway networks. Our home was not in the immediate danger zone, but Father made the decision that we should move into one of the camps outside the city in the countryside where we would be safer from any stray bombs that might fall on our neighbourhood. I didn't want to leave our house, but Father insisted there could be no arguing over it. I recall my mother gathering up all her items of jewellery and packing them and clothes into cases. We children did the same, packing our cases as full as we could get them with warm clothes. We left the house and Father organized some transport to take us out of the city. In the countryside farmers gave up barns and haylofts, and tents were erected in an effort to cater for as many people as was possible. It was a real community spirit at these camps which gave us refuge from the bombs. Some of the tents were erected in the woods and these were very nice in summer when the leaves were on the trees but unpleasant in the winter weather and rain. We were lucky enough to be billeted in a nice cosy hayloft just across the yard from a large farmhouse. The hayloft had a secure roof which didn't leak when it rained, and it was made very comfortable for us with blankets and sacking with which we made our sleeping quarters. There were around thirty other people in the hayloft which you had to climb a ladder to get into. In an emergency such as a fire there was another bigger door at the other end of the hayloft through which to escape. No one was permitted to smoke in the hayloft for obvious safety reasons. This new safer environment brought about an air of complacency. I often took my siblings out into the pasture where there was a pond which was alive with croaking frogs and toads in it in the summertime. We would spend many hours here with the other kids.

One unforeseen problem with the camps was the combination of poor sanitation and the outbreak of infections. The camps were as comfortable as they could be made yet the winter of 1944/5 was very cold with much of the country blanketed in heavy snow. Through that winter most of the young were put in the hayloft where the hay and blankets provided the best warmth. Yet, a few newborn babies soon perished in these conditions. Outbreaks of serious colds and flu also took their toll on those of us in the camps. Food was in very short supply and had to be prioritized and given to those most in need. There was a little milk but many of the cows that had once provided an ample supply had died due to lack of animal feeds. When such a valuable animal died it wasn't wasted: it was butchered for meat and those who cooked for us in the camp used it in soups. Nothing at all went to waste and every part of the animal was used. Allied fighter aircraft sometimes came over the fields and machine-gunned cattle and horses. They knew these animals could be considered an aid to the German war effort and were considered fair game. Fresh carcasses were cut up into joints and often salted or dry-cured in an attempt to preserve them. The workers on the farms were very good at this and their knowledge and skill undoubtedly saved many of us from starvation. I recall the boys of the Hitler Youth – some of them had pistols on their belts but they had no ammunition for them, so they were useless – made themselves catapults by breaking parts of trees and carving them with their knives. Once they had got the basic shape they would then go and look for something like elastic to act as the sling which would fire a glass marble, stone or pebble. Rubber was very hard to come by and was recycled wherever possible, so finding suitable material wasn't easy. When an Allied aircraft was shot down nearby the boys would go out to it and look for anything they could use and sometimes they would come back with things they could use to build their catapults. These primitive weapons required a high degree of skill to shoot accurately and the skill levels of the Hitler Youth boys was pretty good as they had been taught these things. Sometimes we were bored and would tag along with them just to watch as they attempted to shoot birds or squirrels from trees. In winter there were not many squirrels to be found as most were in hibernation inside tree trunks. The boys would still hunt them though by poking a stick in through a hole in a tree to see if anything was inside. If there was, the creature would be driven out and dealt a blow with a stick or shot with one of the catapults. I remember one boy shot a pigeon using a glass marble. He pulled the elastic of his catapult right back and when he let the shot go it hit the bird with a loud thumping sound and feathers went in all directions. The bird hung upside down for a few seconds, its feet still gripping the branch it had been sitting on, then it dropped to the ground. Squirrels were a much harder target. Once driven out of their nests they would run up to the higher branches but would run up the opposite side of the tree so you could not see them. I remember one morning a squirrel had been driven out and it shot up the tree and one of the other boys went around the side instructing the boy with the catapult where the animal was and where he should get ready to aim. It came around our side of the tree, momentarily stopping, and *thwack* – the boy let go with his catapult which struck the squirrel in its body. I could hear it squeaking in pain as it clung onto the branch of the tree. The boy was just reloading another marble when the squirrel's grip relaxed, and it fell to the ground. When the squirrel hit the ground, we all gathered around it. One boy made the big mistake of picking up the wounded rodent which then sank its sharp teeth into his hand. He was then squealing out in pain and we all laughed at his misfortune while another boy dealt the squirrel the coup de grâce with a stick. If you were lucky, on a good morning

Annie and Karl Krause, Herti's parents on their wedding day, 26 June 1927.

ANDRITZ bei GRAZ.
W. Kramer 197.

ndritz near Graz. Herti's house is at the bottom left corner. When the roof blew off it landed next
the restaurant opposite, seen on the right.

Herti in her pram with her parents.

Herti aged 2 on Myra, 1931.

Herti and her grandfather in Laxenburg, bakery delivery, 1931.

erti's father Karl in his police uniform on the extreme left.

rti with her parents.

Herti – Christmas, 1932.

Herti with her parents. Herti is wearing a sailor suit she wore in a fashion show.

Herti in her sailor suit.

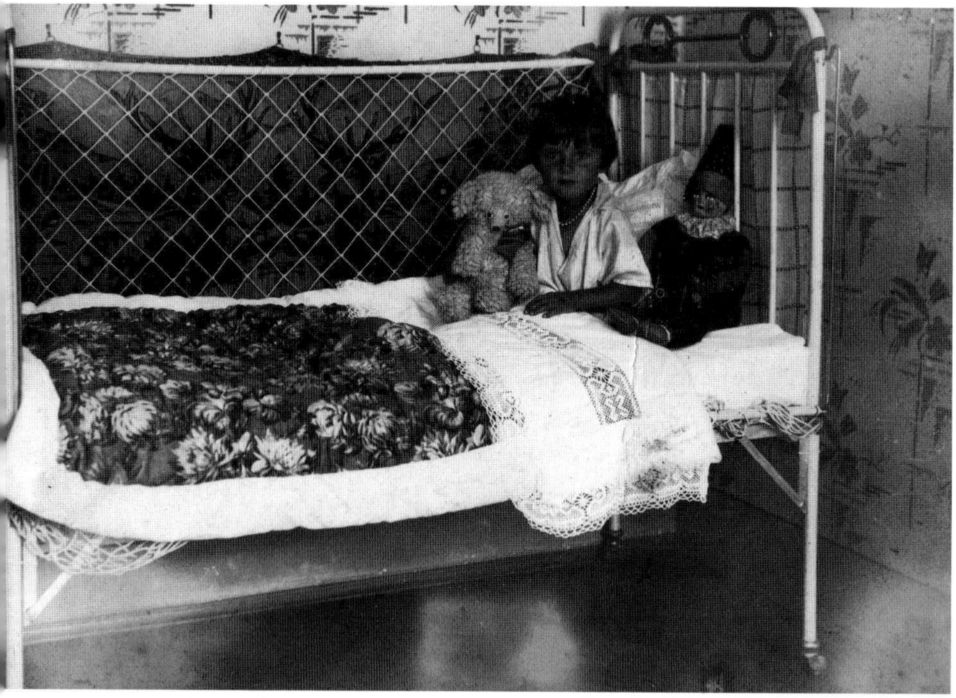

rti in her bed with her toys.

Herti with her uncle Rudi whose family had a
vineyard where the family was later attacked.

Herti with her parents at her first Holy Communion aged ten.

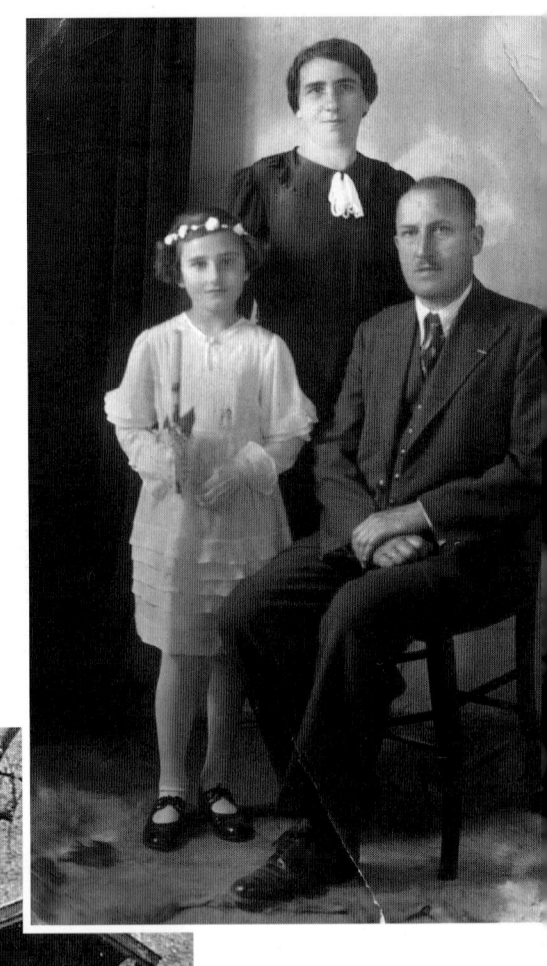

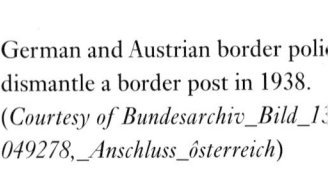

German and Austrian border poli
dismantle a border post in 1938.
(*Courtesy of Bundesarchiv_Bild_1*
049278,_Anschluss_ôsterreich)

Hitler crosses the border into Austria, March 1938. (*Photo courtesy of Wikipedia via private collection of H. Blair Howell*)

Seyss-Inquart and Hitler and Heydrich (on right) in Vienna, March 1938. (*Courtesy of the Bundesarchiv_Bild_119-5243,_Wien,_Arthur_Sey·-Inquart,_Adolf_Hitler*)

Supporters of Schuschnigg campaigning for the independence of Austria in March 1938, shortly before the Anschluss. (*Wikipedia*)

Ubungs Schule, Hasner Platz, Graz Class Photo. Herti is fourth from the left, middle row. The girl marked with an 'X' vanished.

Gerta Nienaus – fate unknown.

Greta Kubkat – fate unknown.

Heidi Muhlbacher – fate unknown.

Gretl Leibgret – fate unknown.

Helga Tragan – fate unknown.

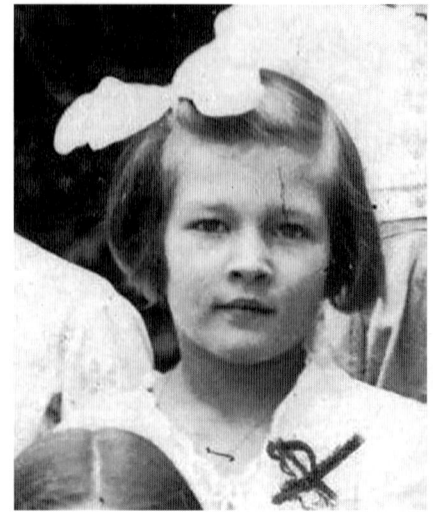

Mitzie Kuschel – fate unknown.

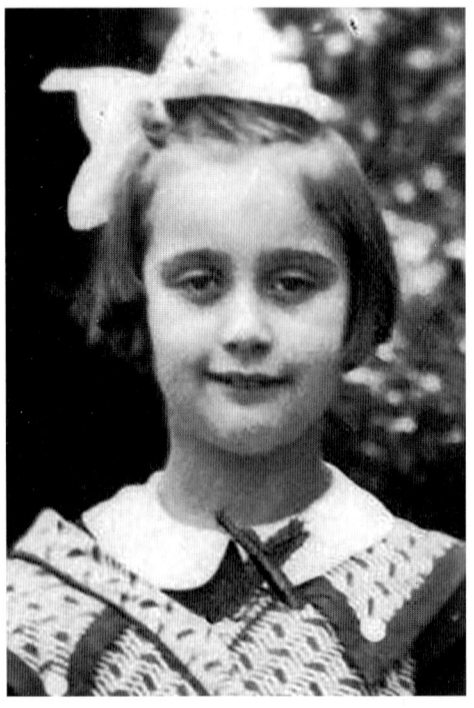

Inge Lyckowetz – fate unknown.

Traudi Haucink – fate unknown.

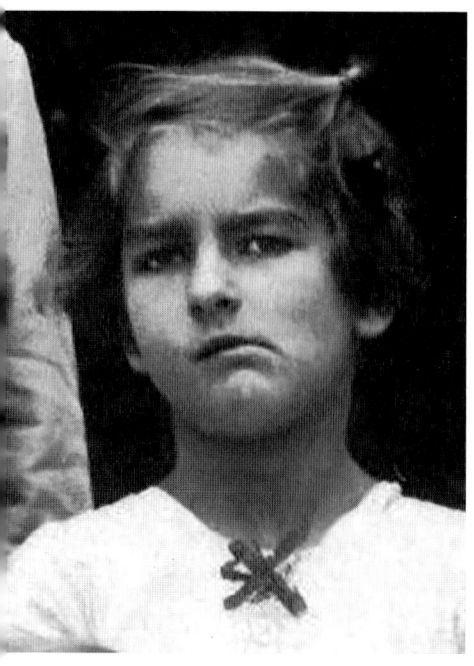

Lori Reichenfelser – fate unknown.

Herti with her toy doll.

An 11-year-old Herti pictured here with a student lodger who stayed at her house around 1941.

A young Amelia 'Milly' Keller digging in the sands at Wansee. (*Courtesy of R. Schildt*)

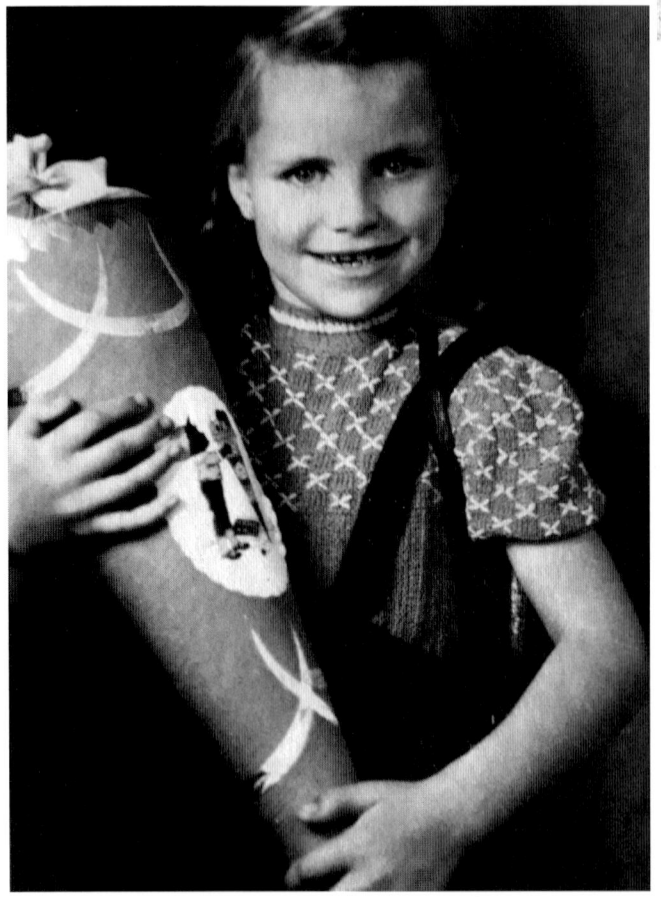

Milly Keller from Innsbruck. Here she is holding her Schultute–Sugar Bag aged 8 starting full-time schooling.

Hilde Schubert pictured here in happier days with her father.

A young Ellie Bergmann. She could actually drive her grandfather's car she is standing by. (*Courtesy of Bergmann family*)

The Galliford family. This photo was taken in Torquay in 1950 and sent to Herti when she had arrived in London.

Herti's identity card issued by the post–Second World War Austrian authorities as proof of her Austrian citizenship.

Herti with her much-loved piano that survived the bombing and was still there when she returned to Graz. This photo was taken shortly before her marriage.

rti outside her home in Hampstead
the 1980s.

Herti's retirement from British Airways in 1986.

Herti (left) with Virginia Wells.

you could bag several pigeons and a couple of squirrels which all went to the camp's food supply. It was funny really, while we were out on these hunting excursions, politics and the war were never discussed. It was like we were doing all the things that children should be doing at that time. Most of the boys were Hitler Youth boys in name only – few of them really believed the Germans were going to win the war especially by that winter of 1944/5. Most of them just wanted it to end so that they could get back to living a normal life again. At that time, we were living a primitive existence, day to day, and waiting for this war to end.

One day, when we were down by the pool catching frogs, I suddenly heard the sound of engines high up in the sky above. As I looked up, at first it was just possible to make out tiny specks and it was difficult to see what these were for a few seconds. I instinctively called my siblings and without question they came running over to me. I was kneeling down by a fallen tree trunk and I told them to get down behind it with me. As I covered their heads I looked up and I could see what I soon recognized as a German Focke-Wulf Fw190 aircraft. The Focke-Wulf was diving down towards us – I could clearly see the big radial engine. He was going full bore, flat out and the sound of his engine straining was testament to the speed he must have been travelling at. I thought he was going to hit the ground before us, but around 200 feet above the ground as I estimated it to be, he pulled up. As he pulled up above us, I felt the blast from his propeller wash, with dust and other small bits of debris flying up into the air and momentarily obscuring my vision. As I wiped my eyes and my vision cleared, I saw the Focke-Wulf climb, roll over and level out just as another aircraft was passing before him. There was the sound of gunfire as the Focke-Wulf fired at the aircraft in front of him which immediately caught fire and fell like a brick into the ground probably a quarter of a mile away from where we were. The Focke-Wulf circled his victim for a few seconds before heading off in an easterly direction. I found out after returning to the camp that the aircraft that had been shot down was an American P-47 Thunderbolt fighter. I didn't see the pilot bale out and his fate remained a mystery to me. No one was permitted to go near the wreckage which remained in the field for some months after 1945, until it was removed. We often saw the streams of bombers passing overhead on their way to bomb Innsbruck. Air battles between American and German fighters could be witnessed frequently. It was far from safe to try and watch these battles as the aircraft were firing in all directions and if you did not take cover you could be hit and killed by accident. So, the same precautions for an air raid were taken whenever any aircraft approached. Several shelters were dug in the surrounding fields and there was a deep cellar beneath the farmhouse and hayloft. After a while it wasn't even safe to go down to the pond and we were told to stay within the perimeter of the farm buildings and never to go off. There had been reports of Allied aircraft strafing civilians on the ground, killing horses, cows, dogs and anything that moved. The dangers were very real, and we heeded the warnings. You always knew when an air battle was taking place in the sky above as the bullet cases, some of which were pretty big, would come falling down. They made a hell of a noise as they hit the corrugated roof of the hayloft. Again, these were quickly collected as souvenirs and by the end of the war I had a grain sack full of German and American cannon and machine-gun cartridge casings. The most common bullet casings we found were the American 12.7mm machine-gun cases or .50 cals as they called them. There were also a lot of German Mauser MG 151 20mm cases, these being fired by the Messerschmitt and Focke-Wulf fighter aircraft. When we left the camp at the end of hostilities, I wanted to take this sack of cartridge cases home with me but my parents wouldn't have it and told me to leave it behind: it may well still be there to this day, I don't know.

Chapter 7

Resistance

As the fortunes of Nazi Germany began their inexorable decline, so a new chapter in Herti's life began to unfold. Herti recalls:

My school was situated near the centre of the city of Graz, facing the River Mur and with its back against a rock fortress. This geographical location was to prove significant as the war progressed, eventually bringing me face to face with 'the enemy' and offering me the chance to try out my language skills.

The first day of the autumn term arrived and I was excited to meet up again with my friends whom I had not seen for the whole of the summer holidays. Like typical teenagers we chatted about our summer activities then, as usual, our day commenced with a game of ball followed by the raising of the swastika flag. During the ten-minute break between lessons I would take advantage of the opportunity to sit on the windowsill of our classroom which overlooked the main road. On this first morning break of the first day of term my attention was drawn to a lengthy column of prisoners marching past the school and it soon became apparent these men were British POWs. Every day I watched out of the window, noticing that they marched past at the same time – early morning break – each day. I had no idea where they were going or why, but I made sure that I was at the window to watch them every morning. Perhaps because of my long hours spent listening to the BBC World Service and my love of the English language I found the whole idea of their proximity very exciting. How I wished for a chance to try out my English! After a while some of the young POWs noticed me watching them and a few of them were brave enough to wave to me! This carried on for the next few months as autumn turned to winter. The Christmas holidays arrived, and we celebrated quietly, missing Father and wondering just how long the war would last.

At the beginning of 1944, the war came closer. I saw the first of the RAF reconnaissance planes from the UK flying over Graz, followed a few days later by a formation of bombers en route to Vienna and also Wiener Neustadt, the location of a large ammunition store. These bombings intensified, becoming more frequent and continued until the end of the war. Graz was under the flight path of these missions and was also a target for the bombers. I realized the implications for our beautiful city and our safety – things were getting a lot more frightening right on our doorstep. I also discovered that the POWs who marched past each day were from a camp situated at Kalsdorf, about thirteen kilometres south of Graz, and that each day they were made to march from the camp to the fortress behind my school. Here they were tasked with digging out tunnels in the rockface to be used as air-raid shelters. The location for these tunnels was ideal – the rocky outcrop was conveniently close to the city centre and the structure of the rock itself was incredibly hard, thus making a very safe shelter. However, the labour involved in the tunnelling must have been extremely arduous and after a long working day the men had another thirteen–kilometre march back to camp. The prisoners were all in their twenties or early thirties, as I recall, and were all British, having been captured in Italy and transported to the camp near Graz; they appeared fit and strong which is probably why they were given this physical labour. However, the work must have taken its toll on their health and I, for one, felt great respect for them and sympathy with their plight. The construction work continued for many months and by the time the bombing raids on Graz itself had intensified there were a few tunnels that were ready to be used as safe air-raid shelters. Since they were literally just behind our school, we had been instructed to use them in the event of a potential bombing attack – we were given detailed directions about how to respond to the air-raid warning sirens, evacuating the school and going directly to our designated shelter for the duration. Once inside the tunnels our lessons would continue until the 'all-clear' was given.

The first time I remember being sent to the tunnels was in early 1944 and was a most frightening experience. We had been studying as normal in our classrooms when the siren sounded – a shockingly loud and horrible noise that chilled us all. In spite of the fear and sense of impending doom there was no panic as we assembled and made our way across the school yard at the rear of the building and crossed the road into the newly created tunnels. Here it felt cold and damp. There was very limited lighting, so the atmosphere was gloomy, sinister and claustrophobic. Gradually my eyes became accustomed to the darkness and I was able to take in more of my surroundings. Straight away I noticed that the POWs were lined up along one side of the tunnel with their backs to the wall. The tunnel was approximately six feet wide and the floor was rough-hewn with large lumps of rock on which the pupils were to sit. We sat in pairs opposite the POWs which left just enough room for the teachers to walk up and down. The lesson continued in the tunnel until the 'all-clear' sounded, the air-raid was over, and it was safe to return to our classroom. Exiting the tunnel this first time we had no idea of what might confront us and neither did we have any idea about what might have happened to our families who perhaps had not had such a safe shelter.

If the sirens sounded when I was not at school – for instance during weekends, holidays or at night-time – we had alternative arrangements in place. Near our house was a chapel, situated a little way up a hillside, and this was the 'safe place' that we went to. This refuge was in a quiet and fairly remote spot and offered security in that it would not be an obvious target. Quite frequently I would go for a pleasant walk up this hill, enjoying the country atmosphere and tranquillity which gave me a chance to relax and escape from some of the stresses of everyday life. One day while I was walking calmly up the hill, I saw a man running out of a house wearing nothing but his wet underpants! An upstairs window was open and from it a young woman was screaming as she threw out various items of clothing. It was in my nature to go and see if the woman was alright, so I went to the house and she let me in. Apparently, the man was a priest who had visited her and she had assumed it was safe to let him in but then he attempted to rape her. However, she had been sufficiently strong to fight him off. I was very impressed by her actions and from this incident I made a new friend – we stayed in touch and I visited her when I went for my walk up the hill and, through my friendship with this remarkable young woman, I became aware of the network of 'safe houses' in the area. I learned that there were many people who were prepared to help those British prisoners trying to escape the oppression and persecution of the Nazis and my thoughts soon turned to the prisoners I had encountered in the tunnels. I have no idea what happened to the priest.

I began to think more and more about the POWs. I anticipated air raids with the hope that I would get close to them and be able to make contact, if only to practise and improve my English conversation, even though I knew that this was strictly forbidden. I looked eagerly for any chance that might arise and fortunately I did not have to wait long. The siren had gone, we were in the tunnels and the teacher's attention was elsewhere: I said a very quiet 'Hello' to one prisoner and was rewarded by his face lighting up, and I knew immediately that these men would welcome interaction with us. After all, if nothing else, here was a group of young, attractive, teenaged girls which would have made a welcome change of company for these soldiers! From then on, we took advantage of any opportunity to exchange whispered conversations and I soon learned that the prisoners' only aim was to escape and get back to England. Naturally, the chances of doing so – especially without assistance – were pretty remote. They asked if there was any possibility that I could help. Over the next few days I mulled over this request and thought hard about just how I might be able to do anything that would make a difference to them. My first thought was that in order to escape they would need civilian clothing and it occurred to me that I could, perhaps, smuggle some of my father's clothes into the tunnels during an air raid. Mother had not disposed of any of Father's belongings after his death – what a blessing this was. At the next opportunity I told the POWs that I believed I could get some clothes for them and asked if this would be helpful. They were excited by the prospect and clearly their spirits were lifted – here was a golden chance to potentially aid escape.

I knew that this scheme was fraught with difficulty – I had mentioned the idea to no one, and I knew I had to keep this entirely to myself, so my conversations had to be kept from not only the teachers but also my fellow pupils. It would have been extremely foolish to involve anyone else as this would not only put them in danger but also expose me to the risk of being betrayed. So, I planned my 'secret mission' to get clothing to the prisoners without a word to anyone. Quietly I took a pair of trousers from Father's wardrobe and folded them as small as possible, placing them in my school satchel. Luck was with me – the siren went that very day. I grabbed my satchel and calmly took it with me as we were evacuated to the tunnels. Waiting for the 'all-clear', I hung back towards the rear of the tunnel so I would be the last one out. In this way I was able to quickly take out the trousers and hand them discreetly to one of the prisoners without anyone noticing. Coming out of the tunnel I breathed a deep sigh of relief, feeling excited and proud that I had been so daring and that the plan had worked so well. This encouraged me to proceed with more clothing 'drops' and over the next few weeks I took many items from Father's 'supply'. I knew there was a good chance that Mother would look and notice the diminishing piles of trousers, jumpers and shirts and I did not want to deceive her, so I told her what I was doing. Fortunately, she felt, as I did, that this was an opportunity to help and she supported my efforts, turning a blind eye to my activities, even though she must have been very worried in case I was caught. Knowing that outer clothing would also be important I managed to take in some jackets which were particularly difficult to get into my satchel and necessitated the removal of a good number of books. Needless to say, every time I 'dropped' an item of clothing the prisoners were very grateful and fulsome in their thanks. I just hoped this would be a useful first step in their ability to escape.

During the time I was smuggling clothes into the tunnels I was also finding out more about safe houses, initially through the contact I had made with my friend who lived up the hill. There was an established network by this time of people living in Graz who were prepared to help British prisoners escape Austria, in spite of great personal risk. Prisoners would be taken to one safe house before being moved to another and another, eventually crossing the border into Yugoslavia from where they hopefully were successful in getting back to England.

So, I started to think if there was any way I could get one of the prisoners in the tunnel out and to a safe house, and ultimately enable him to get home. With the help of my friend who lived on the hill, I managed to make contact with one of the 'safe house' people and it was agreed that I would try to bring a prisoner to them. Next, I had to set about making a plan that would work and put my proposal to the prisoners themselves. I told them my idea and that I would be willing to try and get one of them to safety, so long as they were wearing some of the civilian clothing that I had previously given them. I imagine there must have been some discussions amongst the prisoners as they marched back to camp that night about the prospect of being successfully escorted to safety by a 15-year-old girl! Still, I had proved I was willing to take risks and was not afraid of a challenge – and I think I must have had quite a mature and cool head on my shoulders. Perhaps they recognized this too as it was soon decided that during an air raid one prisoner would try to remain behind in the tunnel after the rest of the workforce had marched back to camp. The young man who volunteered for this risky enterprise was called Leslie and he was, as I remember, a very handsome, blond young soldier! He said he would change his clothing, hide and wait until I was able to return to the tunnel entrance and collect him. His fellow prisoners would cover for him as long as possible in order that the escape method should remain a secret. This might not have been too difficult as the guards were all older Austrian men who were not young or fit enough for active service so had been conscripted for supervision duties. However, they, too, had to complete the twice-daily march to and from the prison camp and would have found their task tiring and demanding so it is reasonable to expect they may not have been particularly vigilant. Also, I am sure no one would have expected a schoolgirl to be involved in assisting prisoners to escape.

After school that day, instead of taking my normal route home, I went back to the air-raid shelter to, hopefully, meet the man. Knowing this venture was full of danger, my heart was pumping, and I dreaded finding my plan had failed. I felt pure joy when I saw him there at the entrance as arranged, dressed in a way that would pass casual scrutiny. I told him to follow me at a safe distance and be vigilant. The safe house where I had planned to take him was situated on the far side of the wide and fast-flowing River Mur, swollen by meltwater from the mountains and which runs through the centre of Graz. The only route across was via the bridge. Unfortunately, German guards were posted at each end of the bridge and we were bound to be challenged. Naturally, at the time the only men wearing 'civvies' were too old to be enlisted so there was a good chance my POW would be discovered. Quickly we discussed the problem and I came up with a plan we thought might work, though of course it was risky. I approached the bridge first and made out that I was 'available', flirting with the soldiers in a way in which I had not known I was capable. It was amazing how quickly they were distracted from their guard duty and, while 'otherwise occupied', my POW was able to climb down the riverbank and slip underneath the bridge. Clutching on to the steel girders supporting the stonework, he was able to get a firm enough grip to pull himself across the river. What luck the current was not too great or the weather too cold. After a while I left these first, disappointed guards and made my way over the bridge to embark on a similar ploy at the other end. Again, it worked a treat – the guards were distracted, and my POW was able to get out of the river and scramble up the bank, through the bushes, to safety – cold and wet but otherwise perfectly all right. Once we were out of sight, we continued the short distance to the safe house, and I handed him over. He thanked me sincerely and we said goodbye – this was the last I saw of him.

By the time I arrived home I had managed to calm down a bit and my heart was not racing as it had on the bridge, even though I am sure I appeared completely in control to the guards. I wonder what they thought after I had left them – probably they had a laugh at the saucy, teasing teenager! I didn't care – I had managed to transfer my man safely and now the rest of his escape would be up to the others in the 'team', and good fortune. I have often wondered about the rest of his journey and if he was successful in getting home and, indeed, if he went on to enjoy a long and happy life.

It wasn't long before I felt it would be worth having another go at helping the prisoners, so I arranged with one of them to meet in the same way as the first.

The British prisoner of war that young Herti was to assist in escaping Austria on this occasion was Sergeant William Gledhill of the Hampshire Regiment, service number 5495853, who was born on 7 March 1913 and who came from Newcastle, England. Generally known as Bill, his POW number was 7422 and he was listed as being held at Stalag 18A.* Herti continues:

All went to plan except that there was a delay in taking Bill to the safe house: a recent bombing raid had caused major structural damage, which had compromised the route, making it impossible to complete the journey. So, what was I to do with Bill? There was only one thing possible and that was to take him home with me. The journey home went relatively smoothly this time, though I had no idea how my mother would react when I took this dangerous stranger into our home and I tried to anticipate what I would do if she was not prepared to help me. It was a massive relief when, after her initial surprise, Mother agreed to support my endeavour: she said Bill could stay in the house for as long as was necessary, even though this placed all of us, including little Mädy, at great risk. I faced a considerable dilemma, too, since I had given my promise to Father that I would protect Mother and Mädy and yet, here I was, exposing them to danger. What would Father have thought of my actions?

---

* Ginny's sister Lucy and nephew Peter carried out some research and confirmed that the camp Kalsdorf bei Graz was, indeed, part of Stalag 18A and that the main Stalag 18A facility was at Wolfsberg. Judenberg was home to KZ Nebenlager-Bretstein, which was a sub-camp of the Mauthausen concentration camp before becoming DP Camp KZ N-B, a camp constructed by Mauthausen prisoners and internees consisting mainly of Spanish nationals and German Jehovah's Witnesses.

Bad luck was with us again, however, as a few days later all women and children were to be evacuated from Graz, since the bombing attacks had increased. From this time on, it became more and more difficult to obtain even very basic food and provisions. Gradually more establishments were closed, and, with the evacuation of the children, the schools ceased to function. Although I did not know it, my own formal education had come to a premature end and, in spite of my academic ambitions, I had effectively left school for good. It was, of course, impossible for us to leave with the other evacuees as our POW was still with us so we had to stay behind and take our chances. Fortunately, the evacuation was voluntary and there were a number of people who chose to stay, including neighbours of ours who were also very good friends. This family owned a restaurant – the Pfleger – which is still there today. They also had a little boy called Franzi who was five years younger than me – I had known him since he was born, and we had been very close. Franzi is also still living there and it is his daughter who now runs the restaurant. Franzi's parents had a smallholding which supplied the business, keeping cows, pigs and chickens as well as having a vegetable garden and orchard. Thanks to their kindness and generosity, we managed to have some supplies of milk and other basic foods. However, what they could give us was limited and food shortage was a serious problem for us, especially as we had an additional mouth to feed.

After a few days, a safe house was offered but by this time we were facing yet another difficulty: two Gestapo officers had been posted opposite our house where they had a good surveillance spot covering the surrounding area. Even though they were supposedly undercover and in plain clothes, their brown coats and hats were no real disguise! We knew we could not move Bill while they were scrutinizing us so closely, so we remained 'holed up' for the next couple of weeks. It was essential that Bill was not seen so he had to literally lie low and not pass in front of a window. We simply had to be patient, wait for a chance to move and hope for the best.

All the shops had closed once the evacuation had taken place so, apart from what our kind neighbours were able to give us, we soon ran out of provisions. Therefore, I had to effectively forage for whatever I could find – I scavenged maize and potatoes from the surrounding fields and apples and other fruit from the orchards. Then one day I noticed from a window at the rear of the house that a train of horse-drawn wagons would regularly travel along the road that ran on the far side of the fields and tramlines delivering supplies to the German army. I watched this for a while, thinking of ways I could acquire some of these provisions. I knew it would be risky since there were three guards positioned at regular intervals along the convoy. It was imperative that I was not caught – if so, I would most certainly be shot. Anticipating the arrival of another convoy, very quietly I left the house and made my way across to the far side of the fields with my bicycle. Arriving at the spot I had identified as offering the best cover, I lay in a ditch hiding myself and the bike as best I could. As the wagons passed, I carefully watched for the guards, who fortunately were older men and who were not too vigilant and appeared to be quite content to doze peacefully. I gauged the right moment to jump up on the back of one cart and knock two boxes into the ditch. Then I jumped down and lay quietly in the ditch until I was certain all the wagons had passed. Cautiously I climbed out of the ditch and went to retrieve my contraband, which I loaded onto my bike and quickly pedalled home. Since this 'operation' had gone off without a hitch I repeated it on several occasions – the only snag being that we never knew what was inside the boxes until we opened them. Once we had a container full of dried eggs and another of very strong dark chocolate, which was horrible, but at least it was food and helped us get over the next few weeks while the Gestapo remained on the hill watching the front of the house.

Every day I had to think of ways to get food or, indeed, any other items we needed just to get by. I had another idea: I had seen the goods trains that arrived in Graz – the railway station was quite close to the centre of the city and not too far from my school. I guessed that some of these trains would be bringing provisions for the troops stationed there so I thought it worth investigating. One day I set off on my bicycle to make the four-mile journey from our suburb of Andritz into Graz. Sure enough, there at the station goods yard were a number of rail trucks at the sidings. They were clearly goods wagons with closed sides and roofs – the doors were on the sides, just like the cattle trucks used to transport prisoners. However, it was immediately apparent that the train had been hit by a bombing raid as roofs had been blasted off and sides were damaged and open. I glanced around: no one appeared to be on guard, so I took a chance and went towards one of the trucks. Carefully I climbed up, pulling myself into the carriage. My eyes took a few moments to adjust to the gloom within. As I inched forward, I stumbled over a lumpy obstruction and fell into the carriage, aware as I tumbled that I had tripped over a human being. Horrified, I forced myself to look more closely and noticed the bodies of two dead German guards. At the time I had no idea how they had died or why they had been left there, but later assumed the bombing of the train must have occurred very recently while the train was here at the siding and the guards were still on board: inevitably with a direct hit they had died in the blast. I was probably the first person to come across this hideous scene of carnage. Though shocked and horrified, I gathered myself and resumed my task – after all, I was there to see what I could find, and I didn't want to leave empty-handed. There were, indeed, provisions to be foraged, so I loaded what I could and quickly went on to check out some of the other carriages. Each one I entered contained the blasted bodies of dead guards and it is this experience that I remember most vividly rather than exactly what I was able to steal. However, I do remember riding my bicycle home laden with as much contraband as I could carry, though I did find this a traumatic experience and I decided then that I would not go back to the station yard.

Eventually the day arrived when I noticed the Gestapo were not to be seen so I waited a few more days to be certain and decided this would be the best time to move Bill to the allocated safe house. Bill dressed in some of my father's clothes and, to complete his 'costume', Mother gave him my father's gold pocket watch, which would not only be of practical use but would also make him look more 'genuine'. In addition, I am sure this gesture showed Bill just how much we cared about him and how much we hoped he would get back home safely. The two of us set off on our journey which was to take us some distance away from the city in a south-easterly direction. The start of our trip took us up the hill opposite the house where the Gestapo had previously been stationed. We had almost reached the top of the hill when two German soldiers carrying rifles stopped us and started to question Bill. Clearly, he was an anomaly, a young man dressed in civilian clothing when pretty much all men of his age were in the armed forces and in uniform. Additionally, Bill spoke no German – at least none that would not have given him away immediately. I had to think fast, and, on impulse, I stepped forward and took control. I told them that he was on sick leave as he had been shot in the mouth and was unable to speak. I prayed Bill would have enough sense of what I had said to remain silent and, thank goodness, it worked. Bill stayed silent, the Germans stood back and, respectfully, saluted him and we went on our way. Yet again, we had had a lucky escape! When we were well out of earshot, I explained to Bill what had been said. Neither of us could believe we had got away with it.

Having reached the brow of the hill we began a long descent towards the safe house in the next valley. I followed the directions I had been given and eventually we arrived at a large house fronted by a huge iron gate. I rang the bell hanging by the gate and after a little while a beautiful young girl, aged about 17, came and opened the gate to let us in. I told her who we were and why we were there, trusting that everything would be fine. She said we were expected and took us into the house and upstairs where we were to meet her father in his office. She knocked on the door and a commanding voice told us to enter. Seated on the far side of an enormous desk was a high-ranking SS officer. My immediate reaction was that we had been caught in a trap and this was the end – clearly Bill felt the same. However, much to our surprise and disbelief this man got up from behind his desk, came quickly round and welcomed us, shaking our hands profusely and saying, 'Please do not worry, I am here to help you.' For some reason we believed this man and were convinced that he did, indeed, wish to help us. In any case, I really had no option but to trust him and to leave Bill with him. I said my farewells to a man who had become a true friend. War had given us this brief opportunity for closeness and to share a terrible and dangerous adventure. I wished him well and hoped that he would be successful in getting home to England and his family.

Much later I learned that he had, indeed, got safely back, journeying southwards with the support of a network of helpers through Yugoslavia and Italy, along the established escape routes. Years later, when I was living in London, I investigated Bill's life and made contact with his family which was a truly rewarding and emotional experience: I met Bill, his wife and sister in a pub in Acton in the early 1950s. He told me about the rest of his journey and expressed his thanks for all we had done to help him. He showed me that he still had my father's watch and considered it a most precious possession. At the time of our meeting I think we were both still too 'raw' and close to the war to speak really freely. When we parted I believe we were both grateful to have had this chance, but the events we had lived through were still too painful to fully confront. Bill and I said goodbye again and, once more, got on with our lives.

Meanwhile, having left Bill with the 'SS officer', I headed home to rejoin my mother and sister back at home in Andritz. They were relieved and overjoyed to see me arrive home safe and sound. Now we had no reason to stay in Graz – we could have left to join the other evacuees outside the city in the relative safety of the countryside. There was no school since the children had left the city therefore no further opportunity for me to continue my escape operations. However, in spite of this we decided to stay in our house and continue to exist as best we could, obtaining food as before and managing from day to day. The bombings thundered on, I cautiously continued to tune into the BBC, and we became a little bit hopeful that the end of the war was in sight.

Resistance however miniscule will flourish wherever a dictatorship takes root within a society. Austria was no exception to this rule, yet the lack of initial resistance to the German invasion of Austria would imply a degree of complicity with the Nazi regime. At the time of the Anschluss there were perhaps many Austrian citizens who were convinced that the benefits of an allegiance with Hitler's Third Reich would far outweigh any negative political or social aspects.

The exact number of individual cases of resistance against the Nazis during their occupation of Austria is very difficult to ascertain. For example, the term 'resistance' can refer to such instances where Austrian citizens listened in to enemy broadcasts on the radio, non-compliance in work duties, making statements liable to undermine the morale of the people and showing kindness towards forced labourers allocated such duties as working in agriculture or in factories. Anyone found guilty of any of the above could face death under National

Socialism. Many will ask the question as to why a greater resistance towards the Germans in Austria did not materialize. The answer to this is quite a simple one: the whole Nazi system was able to establish its stranglehold over the people of Austria due to the fact that many citizens actively supported the regime through all professions and walks of life, from teachers, students, block wardens, neighbours, publicans to the ordinary man and woman on the street. This meant that any signs of dissent or derogatory remarks made against the regime would easily reach the ears of the Nazi authorities who would then investigate without hesitation. Those citizens who had their suspicions of anyone partaking in resistance activities who did not report them to the authorities were themselves also guilty of the crime. All the evidence required to prove that there was a highly efficient clandestine resistance movement in operation in Austria is given by Herti through her account: she was indeed a young girl who risked her life (and that of her family) to assist 'the enemy'. The sheer selfless bravery of individuals such as Herti cannot be commended highly enough. It is believed that some 100,000 Austrian citizens became involved in various acts of resistance. Thousands were rounded up by the authorities and were either executed or imprisoned. Among the silent heroes of the Austrian resistance were Rosa Stallbaumer (1897–1942) and her husband Anton. Rosa and her husband became active within the Austrian resistance shortly after the Anschluss. They provided a hiding place for Jewish people who had been targeted by the Nazis and helped a number of Jews escape from Vienna to Italy by way of Austria's East Tyrol region. The couple were betrayed by Nazi sympathizers in 1942, after which they were soon arrested by the Gestapo. After being charged, Anton was then sent to Dachau concentration camp. According to camp records, Anton Stallbaumer arrived at the camp on 10 October 1942 as a political prisoner being assigned his inmate number of 289406. The camp records also stated that Anton Stallbaumer had been in residence at Sillian, Austria, at the time of his arrest and he had been born in that community on 8

May 1888. The couple had two young daughters aged 9 and 14 who, having endured the trauma of their parents being incarcerated, were then forcibly separated from each other before being sent to different Nazi 're-education' camps. Rosa was sent to the infamous Auschwitz concentration camp in Poland, thus ensuring that she and her husband remained separated for the duration of their imprisonment. Anton, quite remarkably, survived his long and difficult period of incarceration at Dachau and was released on 14 December 1943. His wife, however, was not so fortunate. Rosa died at Auschwitz on 23 November 1942, and while Anton had been notified of his wife's death by Nazi officials, no circumstances regarding her death were given. The two daughters were later reunited with their father. The youngest of the two girls had been placed in the care of a Slovenian farmer during the period of her parents' imprisonment. Following Anton's release from Dachau, he returned to Austria with his two girls. It was only after their highly emotional reunion that Anton was able to tell his two girls that their mother had died at Auschwitz. In the years following the end of the war Anton attempted to re-build his family. He remarried and died in Sillian, Austria, on 20 October 1962. Anton's and Rosa's eldest daughter Luise Reider (née Stallbaumer) recalled the painful memories she had of her parents at that time, of her father being taken away by the Gestapo in the May of 1942, and of spending a brief time with her mother two days afterwards at a Mothers' Day celebration. Rosa Stallbaumer's name is one of 124 men and women from Tyrol inscribed on the Liberation Monument at the Eduard-Wallnofer-Platz in Innsbruck recognizing those who perished as a result of resisting the Nazi regime in Austria.

There was also a degree of resistance from within the Wehrmacht itself: Robert Bernardis, Heinrich Kodre, Major Carl Szokoll (who was involved in the 20 July plot to kill Hitler), Major Karl Biedermann, Hauptmann Alfred Huth and Oberleutnant Rudolf Raschke all joined in the resistance movement of Austrian members of the Wehrmacht. The group was led by Major Carl Szokoll, within the Wehreiskommando XVII.* It was in the spring of 1945 the group began planning Operation Radetzky. Their plan was to assist the Soviet Army in the liberation of Vienna and to prevent any major destruction of the city. Biedermann was, with the assistance of his troops, to occupy key positions in the city in order to prevent the destruction of vital bridges. The planned date for the implementation of Operation Radetzky was 6 April 1945. However, the group was betrayed: Robert Bernardis, Heinrich Kodre, Karl Biedermann, Alfred Huth and Rudolf Raschke were arrested, sentenced to death by the Volksgerichtshof (People's Court) and executed the same day.

Another little-known hero of the Austrian resistance was the Austrian Catholic Franz Jagerstatter. Jagerstatter was a simple peasant from St. Radegund situated in the Innviertel region, which lies close to the birthplace of Adolf Hitler in Braunau, Upper Austria. He was drafted into the Wehrmacht in 1940, yet after completing weeks of his basic training was released from duty as his work on his farm was considered too important. In 1943 he was again called up for military service, but on this occasion he refused, stating his strong religious objections. He was forced to stand trial and, speaking in his own defence on 6 July 1943 in the Reich Military Court in Berlin, he said:

Only in the past year have I become convinced that as a devout Catholic I would be unable to engage in any active military service. It would be impossible for me to be a Catholic and at the same time be a National Socialist. When I complied with the earlier conscription order, I did so because at that time I considered it a sin not to obey state orders. Now, however, God has given me the thought that it is not a sin to refuse service in the armed forces. There were matters in which I was obliged to obey God more than man; the commandment 'Thou shalt love thy neighbour as thyself' forbids me to engage in armed service, though I am prepared to serve as a paramedic.

---

* lit. Hunting Commando.

The words of this brave man were dismissed as treachery by the military court and Franz Jagerstatter was executed by guillotine at a prison in Brandenburg an der Havel, close to Berlin on 9 August 1943, his only crime being a conscientious objector. Jagerstatter's refusal to serve in the German armed forces was in its day one of the most prominent acts of defiance and resistance from an ordinary Austrian farmer. Quite apart from his acts of resistance he also voiced disgust at the war crimes being committed on the Eastern Front by the German military. This was long before anyone dared to publicly voice opposition to what became known as the Holocaust. His actions therefore contradicted the spurious claims by some Austrian citizens that they had no prior knowledge of Nazi war crimes in the wake of the Second World War. It is sad that this brave man's deeds for a great many years have remained largely undocumented even in Austrian resistance records. Thankfully, on 26 October 2007, the Vatican through the Bishop of Linz, beatified Franz Jagerstatter, bestowing upon him the halo of martyrdom from the Catholic Church. It is also ironic that the bishop's predecessor had attempted to dissuade Jagerstatter from sacrificing his own life for his faith during the Second World War, and instead align himself with the Nazis as the Catholic Church hierarchy had done at the time. Today Jagerstatter is recognized as one of the most courageous of the Austrian resisters of the Second World War, though his recognition as with many others was long overdue. His 'non-performative protest' has been highlighted in Terrence Malick's film *A Hidden Life*, released in January 2020.

Another case worthy of mention is that of the lovers Elfriede Hartmann and Rudolf Masl who were both members of the Austrian Communist youth resistance in Austria. Both fell foul of the Nazi authorities for collecting and disclosing German military secrets as part of their resistance activities. Such acts of treason are, in the military's view, among the worst offences any soldier can commit. During the Second World War the Germans meted out severe punishments to any persons disclosing or divulging such information to the Allies. Rudolf Masl, who was serving with the Wehrmacht in Norway, collected field post addresses of the German units in an effort to carry out what has been termed 'undermine defence'. From what information was to hand at the time of writing it is believed that Rudolf Masl's girlfriend Elfriede 'Friedl' Hartmann began to archive a large bundle of German field post addresses in a secret stash in Vienna. The idea behind this was to then send bogus letters and anti-German propaganda flyers to these German units in an effort to undermine their morale. Elfriede's father was a Jew and thus she had been denied the right to continue her studies under the Nazis. When the two were compromised by the Nazi authorities Elfriede managed to smuggle dozens of secret messages from the Gestapo jail to her family in order to try and save her boyfriend's life. One of her secret messages (or *Kassibers* as they were referred to) was delivered to her parents on 9 September 1941, when they announced that they would be present outside the courtroom where the main trial against her and another defendant was to take place. In it she begged them to: 'Please eat a proper and big breakfast; you have to force yourselves. So that when I leave the judgement hall, and I have to tell you "Death", you do not collapse. Get a hold of yourselves and be strong. I know what I have fought for, with the awareness that if I rest, there will be no salvation for me. I was always aware of that. For me the verdict is not difficult. So, my dear ones, courage, courage – I still live on.' Elfriede's words to her parents are powerful, exemplifying her sheer bravery in the face of certain death. Elfriede Hartmann and Rudolf Masl were executed on 27 August and 2 November 1943 respectively. For Elfriede Hartmann, the love she had for her Wehrmacht soldier boyfriend Rudolf Masl, along with her political engagement against what she viewed was a war of destruction of the Wehrmacht and SS, were inseparable from each other. The following lines penned by a Turkish author served as Elfriede's motto and read:

> If I don't burn,
> If you don't burn,
> How will the light vanquish the darkness?

Herti herself was officially recognized for her selfless bravery in assisting a British prisoner of war to escape from Austria back to England. After the war had ended in 1945, Herti's mother received a letter. When she opened it, she discovered that it contained a letter signed by King George VI of Britain, thanking her for helping British POWs escape to England. Herti never saw the letter herself as she was working away from home at the time. She assumed that the man she helped escape, Bill, had been debriefed upon his return to England on the details of his escape and reported that he could not have escaped without the support of both Herti and her mother.*

---

* There is a good chance that if a copy of this document exists it could be filed and held by the National Archives here in the UK. Sadly, time has not permitted any research into this, yet it is something Herti can be rightly proud of.

Chapter 8

The Russian Terror

M eanwhile, Herti, her mother and sister continued to survive day to day as best they could whilst the Allied bombing intensified and the hoped-for end to hostilities approached. Herti recalls:

There have been a few occasions in my life when my dreams have come true. Once was shortly before my beloved father died, I dreamed that this terrible thing would happen and shortly before the events I am about to relate occurred I had another of these dreams. I woke suddenly from a disturbed sleep in which I witnessed the bombing of our home – in my dream I clearly saw it was a Sunday lunchtime just after we had finished our meal. The dream was so vivid I felt sure it must be portentous.

We had continued to live as best we could over the weeks and months, existing on whatever food we could get our hands on and whatever I could find on my foraging expeditions. The bombing attacks continued both day and night and we spent many hours in the basement which we used during air raids. However, a few days after I had my dream, one Sunday, at about one o'clock, the siren sounded just as we were about to have our lunch. Because we were at home Mother, Mädy and I made our way to the basement to take shelter from the bombing. Our basement was accessed by a flight of stairs inside the house that went to the cellar although this part of the house was only slightly below ground level and there were also some outside steps that led down to an external cellar entrance. Once we were safely 'below stairs' I went to the outside door to look and see if there were any planes going overhead. Sure enough, a number of aircraft appeared and the noise of their engines increased as they came closer. I watched them as their path came directly over Andritz and fully expected them to continue on their journey north towards Vienna (they would have left their bases in the south, probably in Italy or Malta) without any danger to us. However, as I watched the sky, focusing my eyes on the underbelly of one aircraft, I saw one solitary bomb emerge. It was long and shaped like a rocket. Horrified, I followed its path as it fell at an angle that seemed to be coming directly towards me. I rushed back inside the cellar, shouting as loud as I could for Mother and Mädy to 'Get down', though they were in fact already flat on the floor with Mother covering Mädy with her own body. Either I threw myself down or the blast itself flung me forward and I landed prostrate on the concrete. Even though we had become accustomed to explosions this was the first time we had received a direct hit and the noise and shock were phenomenal, as the whole building shook and a massive gaping crack opened up in the concrete just inches away from our eyes. The bomb itself had landed in the garden right against the outside wall of the house, causing a massive crater, and the force of the blast had taken off the roof which was lying in pieces in the neighbouring orchard that belonged to our friends who owned the restaurant. After the shock, we emerged to see what damage had occurred, simply relieved that we were together and unhurt, apart from ringing in our ears and some bruises and scratches sustained as we fell in a pile on the floor. Our house was still standing but without a roof it would not be possible to remain living here so we packed up our belongings, shut the house as securely as possible and went to live in a friend's house about a hundred yards away, which they had left during the earlier evacuation and which they were only too pleased for us to use.

This house provided us with shelter and remained our family home until sometime after the war ended in the spring of 1945. However, we managed to return to our own damaged house between air raids to try and do as much as possible to carry out repairs and to fetch clothing and other items while we stayed in our temporary accommodation. I listened carefully to the news of the liberation of Europe but, of course, the situation in Austria was far from simple.

Hilde Schubert began to have what she referred to as a 'bad feeling about things' the moment her father stopped sending letters from the Eastern Front. Hilde recalls:

We had no real idea of what was going on or why my father's letters had ceased. Father wrote to us frequently to give us some slight reassurance that he was okay. So, when his letters became more sporadic, then suddenly stopped, we were very afraid for what might have happened to him. We were not having the easiest of times in Vienna, especially from 1944 when the Allied bombing of the city increased. Luckily for us our home was not located near the centre of the city, though the nearest bombs that fell by us were just a street away. We were also now living on very little food and it fell to me and Katrin to go out scavenging for anything we could bring home to eat. We were out on one of our scavenging forays one afternoon in December of 1944. It was a cold, dreary day and we felt it was safe for us to go out and look for any scraps of food. Often we would steal food items from military storage points, but this became very risky in the later war years and you could be shot for it. So we had to devise another plan to try and get something to eat. Katrin was such a pretty girl she felt that she may be able to bribe some of the soldiers guarding the military rations. So, off we went to the storage point where we knew the rations were consolidated before being shipped out to the troops. Katrin would strike up a conversation with one of the young soldiers on guard while I would stand by her side pretending to be upset and cry. One soldier fell for our ruse but only after procuring a lingering kiss from Katrin. It was amusing as the young guard looked around first to make sure no one else was nearby or looking so he didn't get into trouble with his superiors. He gave us a few things but was very nervous and told us to leave soon afterwards. We told him we could come back in a few days' time and see him again. Three days passed and we went back again and began to talk to the young guard. He actually seemed very nice and we learned that his name was Willi and that he was just an ordinary soldier. In fact, we got to know him well and he not only gave us food items but told us what was going on in the war against Russia. We told him our father was a soldier away in the east somewhere and had not written to us for a long time and we were worried about him. It was then Willi told us that things were very bad in the east and that maybe our father's unit was cut off and so mail would not get out from the battlefront. Both Katrin and I felt that Willi was being conservative with the truth but understood he could have been shot if caught giving us supplies or telling us anything he shouldn't. We grew to like him and felt that he was just another human being caught up in this war – that he was not an enthusiastic soldier. This did figure as he was only 21, just a boy really. Christmas that year was dismal in every respect: we had no decorative tree, little food and no presents to give each other. Keeping warm and safe were constant hardships for us, but we were resilient. It was one day after Christmas 1944 that we had our first real shock and a sense of impending doom coming our way. Katrin and I were out on one of our forays when we heard the sound of engines approaching. Katrin looked around trying to find where the planes were coming from. She grabbed my hand and we both instinctively crouched down against the ground. Seconds afterwards six aircraft came overhead. They were green-painted and what startled us was the fact that they had big red stars beneath their wings and on their sides. There wasn't a German aircraft to be seen and we hadn't seen any for some weeks. The Russian planes roared overhead followed by the sounds of explosions seconds later. They had dropped bombs most likely onto the storage areas where we had been scavenging. Katrin took my hand again and we ran home to tell our mother what we had seen. She was very alarmed at our story but like most of the inhabitants of the city we didn't know quite what to do – whether to stay or leave.

The ominous sight of Russian aircraft over the city of Vienna, as witnessed by Hilde and Katrin, was indeed all they needed to know that things were far worse than anything that the Nazi propaganda machine was admitting to. The Vienna Offensive, as it was called by the Red Army, began on 2 April 1945. Following the failure of the Unterhehmen Fruhlingserwachen, or Operation Spring Awakening, the German 6th SS Panzer Army under the command of Waffen SS-Oberst-Gruppenfuhrer Sepp Dietrich had retreated in stages to the Vienna area. The German forces in and around Vienna desperately began to create defences around the city with which to meet the now rapidly advancing Red Army.

Hilde Schubert and her family noticed that German soldiers were now falling back into the city in ever greater numbers and watched them as they dug trenches and constructed anti-tank defences. Hilde recalls:

We knew this was it, as they say – the last stand of our city. The last time Katrin and I saw the German soldier, Willi, he warned us to take whatever we had and find the safest place indoors as a battle would soon be taking place between the defending German forces and the Red Army. The fact that he appeared frightened caused us to feel great fear. When we returned home, we told our mother what Willi had said and we began to barricade the windows of our home with our beds and furniture. Katrin and I dragged our beds and mattresses down the stairs and used them to cover the windows and back door to our house. We would 'hole ourselves up' in one corner of our living room and place tables and chairs around us for protection from what might be coming our way. I heard rumours that some homes had placed white flags on sticks outside but was advised not to do so as the authorities were threatening execution for anyone caught doing this. We had suffered air raids and bombs on our city but soon the sound of guns in the distance could be heard. From that time on we only went outside if we really had no choice; otherwise we stayed 'holed up' in our living room where we felt relatively safe.

By the spring of 1945, Russian General Fyodor Tolbukhin's 3rd Ukrainian Front had advanced through western Hungary gathering momentum on each side of the River Danube. After taking Sopron, a Hungarian city located on the Austrian border near Lake Neusiedl, and Nagykanizsa, a Hungarian city in south-western Hungary, the 3rd Ukrainian Front crossed the border into Austria. When the battle for Vienna opened on 2 April 1945, the radio station in Vienna issued a denial that the Austrian capital had been declared an open city. The term 'open city' implies that all defensive efforts have been abandoned in order to avoid the destruction of a city and death or injury to its citizens. That same day, 2 April, Red Army troops were approaching Vienna from the south after overrunning Wiener Neustadt, Eisenstadt, Neunkirchen and Gioggnitz. South Baden and Bratislava were overrun by the Red Army two days later on 4 April. Having arrived in the Vienna area, the 3rd Ukrainian Front surrounded the city and effectively a siege situation developed. Red Army forces were then able to direct their artillery fire into the city while the Red Air Force flew ground-support and bombing sorties over the city. For the besieged inhabitants of Vienna this was just the beginning of the terror to come.

Red Army units involved in the operations to take Vienna were the Soviet 4th Guards Army, 6th Guards Tank Army, 9th Guards Army and 46th Army. The Austrian '0-5 Resistance Group', which had been in existence from 1934 and was violently opposed to Austrofascism, actively participated in acts of sabotage against the German defences in the city to aid the entry of the Red Army into the city. The group, led by Carl Szokoll, had hoped that by doing this both property and life would be spared by the invading Soviet forces.

The only major German force facing the Red Army onslaught was that of the II SS Panzer Corps of the 6th SS Panzer Army. Augmenting this were the scattered remnants of garrison and anti-aircraft units. The anti-aircraft units equipped with deadly 88mm Flak guns would prove formidable opposition against ground targets including tanks. The defence of Vienna lay with General Rudolf von Bunau, with the II SS Panzer Corps units under the command of SS General Wilhelm Bittrich.

However, the Red Army experienced mixed fortunes. In certain areas the Soviets were met with fierce resistance from the defenders, while elsewhere the Red Army was able to advance without opposition. In much of the city, however, most of the fighting was at close quarters. The opposing sides fought with everything at their disposal: rifles, bayonets, pistols, grenades, anti-tank weapons, knives, entrenching shovels and even bare hands. Fierce fighting was soon raging throughout the city and the sounds of battle could be clearly heard by civilians hiding in their cellars. Hilde Schubert recalls:

I can remember the sound of artillery shells falling all over the city. They always used artillery barrages first – it was a sign that the Russians were coming. The sound of a major battle is like nothing you can easily explain. The noise is immense, and you can hear men being killed, you can hear their dying cries as they call out for help. I remember hearing German cries of '*Mutter, Mutter*' (Mother, Mother). A dying man always calls out for the comfort of his mother even when he knows she will never come to be at his side as his life ebbs away from him. The sounds of the fighting become unbearable – you just want it to stop. I remember we all huddled together and Katrin covered my ears even though her lithe fingers could not drown out the noise surrounding us.

Ellie Bergmann recalled the sounds of war approaching her doorstep:

It was like outside there was this eternal thunderstorm raging day and night with the whistle of bombs and shells falling. The Germans were now engaged in a battle with the Russians. My mother and I sought refuge in the cellar of our home. We took what we had which included some warm coats and some candles and matches and went down the stairs into this large room below the house. We were very frightened as the sounds of war, which were still very audible, raged on outside above the ground. We could make out the faint sound of people shouting, but it was difficult to discern whether these voices were German or Russian, civilian or soldiers, we didn't know. All we could do was wait to see what would happen next. Our minds were full of horror stories of marauding hordes from the east who were going to do terrible things to us. Oh, yes, we knew what was coming but what on earth could we have done to escape? It was now far too dangerous to think about going outside and trying to escape. Mother, whose name was Magda, and I just sat huddled together with only the flickering light of a candle with which to provide some light.

In Vienna's second district lies the Prater which is a large public recreation ground and park. It was here that the 6th Panzer Division had made its defensive position. To the south of the city were the 2nd and 3rd SS Panzer Divisions and to the north was the Führer Grenadier Division. These German units comprised the most dedicated and fanatical fighters and these areas soon resembled a slaughterhouse. The Red Army's 4th and 9th Guards Armies were tasked with assaulting Vienna's eastern and southern suburbs. It was here in the eastern suburbs that Hilde Schubert and her family had their first experience of the Red Army. Hilde recalls:

> We heard the Russian soldiers outside our house – there was a lot of shouting, then we heard them battering their way through the front door of the house which we had barricaded. Using the butts of their weapons they smashed a hole through the front door, pieces of wood splintered away and flew through the air. They continued battering down the front door and then four of them burst in. Two of them immediately began searching upstairs and we could hear them throwing things around and shouting to each other as they rummaged through our things, probably looking for valuables. The other two Russians came into the living room and looked around, gesturing for us all to stand up. They looked around our hiding place and prodded the chairs and upturned sofa with the bayonets on the ends of their rifles. After they were satisfied that there were no German soldiers hiding anywhere in the house, they gestured for us to get back down or to stay, I'm not sure which, but we got back down to where we had been hiding. These Russians must have been the spearhead as they didn't hang around and soon moved on. We felt a slight sense of relief that they hadn't harmed any of us as we feared that they might. Yet, our concerns were soon founded over the next few hours when more Red Army soldiers arrived and barged into our house. Again, we stayed down as they searched our house. One of them stood urinating in our hallway though we could all see him, and he made no effort to hide himself as he did this. My mother covered the younger ones' eyes as she didn't want them to see him. Katrin and I looked on in disgust. When he finished, he went into the kitchen and we could hear him looking around for any food. The friend of the Russian who had urinated virtually

in front of us stood looking intently at me and Katrin. He then gestured for the two of us to stand up. At first, we ignored his request until he pulled an angry face and shouted something in Russian and again gestured for me and Katrin to stand up. We thought it was a good idea to obey him this time as we were afraid of what he would do if we ignored him a second time. We stood up and he came closer. Then he grabbed Katrin by her arm and pulled her towards him. He then tried to kiss her, and she pulled away. He then tried to drag Katrin out of the room and was trying to drag her up the stairs. Mother and I jumped up like two angry cats and threw ourselves at this man. We just tried to get him away from Katrin as we knew what his intentions were. The Russian's friend, the one who had been urinating in the hallway, raised his rifle at us and began shouting. For a few seconds there was a lot of commotion, shouting and screaming from us and the Russians when suddenly one Russian drew his pistol and fired a shot up at the ceiling. Pieces of plaster and dust fell down and covered us all. There was this deathly silence apart from the cries from our younger siblings who were all shaking with terror by this point. My mother shouted at them, 'Why don't you go? Leave us alone, we have done nothing to you!' The Russians would not have understood what she had said but the tone of her voice was probably enough. Their intent was still very much there and, while three of the Russians then aimed their weapons at our heads, one again grabbed Katrin by her arm and pulled her towards the stairs. As Katrin was led away up the stairs she told us, 'It will be okay, don't do anything stupid or they will kill us all.' Katrin was taken up into our parents' bedroom and we knew from all the sounds which we could clearly hear from down below that he was raping her. When he had finished, he came down the stairs, grabbed his rifle and pointed it at us while the next one went up and raped Katrin. This went on until all four of these foul creatures had taken their turns on my beautiful sister.

Only then did they leave our house and leave us alone, for the time being at least. The minute those creatures went out the door Mother and I ran up the stairs to find Katrin crying on the bed. They had ripped off her clothing and she was completely naked. Her nose had a small trickle of blood running from it and her arms and wrists were bruised from where she had been pinned down. From this point on I hated them [the Russians]. I hated them more than the Nazis. We did what we could to comfort Katrin, but it was very difficult for us. I couldn't stop crying, Mother was trying hard to be strong for us all, but I could see the strain of it all was slowly breaking her.

The defending German forces kept the Red Army out of the city's southern suburbs until 7 April, though the Soviets were able to gain several footholds before moving into the western suburbs on 8 April with the 6th Guards Tank Army and the bulk of the 9th Guards Army. As the tanks of the 6th Guards Army advanced, they fired on buildings in their path to neutralize any hidden German positions. The western suburbs were the most highly prized due to the fact that this area included Vienna's main railway station. The defenders made determined efforts to thwart the Soviet advance on the station but to no avail: they were outnumbered and outgunned. The western suburbs were soon under Red Army control and later that same day the Red Army began infiltrating both the eastern and northern suburbs. From north of the Danube the Soviet 46th Army pushed its way westwards through Vienna's northern suburbs, effectively cutting off central Vienna from the rest of Austria. On 9 April 1945, Red Army troops began pushing into central Vienna, although progress was relatively slow due to intense street fighting which raged for several days. On 11 April, the 4th Guards Army stormed the Danube canals, with the 20th Guards Rifle Corps and 1st Mechanized Corps advancing on the Reichsbrucke Bridge which was a major artery in Vienna. In what was described as a 'coup de main', on 13 April, the Danube Flotilla landed troops of the 80th Guards Rifle Division and 7th Guards Airborne Division on both sides of the bridge, neutralizing demolition charges which had been laid by the Germans, thus securing the bridge. However, there were other bridges of logistical significance to the Red Army which were destroyed. Vienna fell when the last German defenders surrendered that same day. That night General Bittrich's II SS Panzer Corps pulled out towards the west in order to escape encirclement by the Red Army.

Nothing could prevent the inevitable fall of Vienna to the Red Army and those Viennese citizens who now found themselves under Soviet control were rightly fearful of what was to come. Ellie Bergmann recalls her first experiences of the Russians as they arrived in her district. She was 12 years old at the time:

My mother and I could hear heavy vehicles driving by our house. Tanks made a very different sound as they passed overhead and were clearly discernible from other kinds of vehicles. We heard the approach of a tank, the screeching and grinding sounds of metal on metal which vibrated through the ground shaking everything. We heard it stop across the street followed by a lot of shouting in Russian. Mother and I huddled closer together as we heard them coming into our house. We knew one of the first places they would look would be here where we were hiding in the cellar. We sat in terror as heavy boots moved around the house above then the sound of the cellar door being opened. The candle began to flicker from the draught and then it went out. We were in almost complete darkness apart from the shaft of light entering through the opened cellar doorway. A torch switched on and scanned the darkness followed by the sound of someone coming down the stairs into the cellar. We could see the silhouette of a man armed with a sub-machine gun and he trained his torch all around the cellar before the light shone directly upon us. The soldier approached cautiously in the darkness and two more followed him down the staircase into the cellar. The one with the torch gestured at us to stand and follow him. He was shouting, '*Ruki vverkh!*' telling us to put our hands up. We did as we were told and made our way up the stairs and out of the cellar. We walked through our house and, as we did, I noticed the portrait of my father in his German Army uniform which was now smashed on the floor. As we went out the door into the street outside, I remember thinking that they knew one of our family was a serving soldier in the Wehrmacht and this might bring us trouble. Outside there was much smoke and some of the houses were burning fiercely. There were people we knew being searched for weapons and then they were put into groups. The Russians watched us impassively. I noticed one had what looked like human excrement all over his greatcoat. The whole mood at the time did not feel immediately hostile and my mother and I began to feel a little less threatened by the Russian soldiers. We were told to join the group of other people from our neighbourhood and then instructed to go this church hall which was only a few hundred metres away, so we all trudged off. As we walked along, I noticed there were no old men in our group. I thought for a minute that this was odd – where were the old men of our neighbourhood? In fact, I even mentioned this to my mother who was just as puzzled. She held me tightly by the hand and just said, 'I don't know.' As we came to the church hall there were two Russians at the doorway checking the women and their daughters before they went in. Some of the young girls were picked out and told to stay outside with the soldiers. Their mothers began to protest very strongly until a gun was pointed at them and they were literally pushed inside through the doorway. You could hear them shouting, 'What are you doing with her? Please give her back to me!' Again, that feeling of terror grew in the pit of my stomach as we approached the doorway wondering what our fates would be. I recognized one of the girls who had been separated from her mother: she was just standing there shaking, yet she looked across at me and managed a smile. I smiled back at her but was worried at what was going to happen to me and Mother when our turn came. As we were about to go through the doorway into the hall I was grabbed by the arm and torn away from Mother's grasp. I immediately began to scream with fear and began kicking and fighting to get away from the man holding onto my arm. I broke free and ran into my mother's arms. This time they tried to take Mother away and we held onto each other so tightly they couldn't break our grip. In the end we were thrown to the ground with these angry soldiers kneeling over us shouting things we didn't understand. One had me by the wrists so I couldn't fight, so I began kicking him instead. Then one of the others came, pushed the soldier away and then sat on top of me and grabbed me by the wrists and held me down on the ground. As I struggled with this man who was sitting on me, I hadn't noticed my mother engaged in her own individual battle. She struck one of the Russians who then slapped her hard across the face, bloodying her nose. Anger and hate surged through me and despite not being able to move my arms, I kicked and kicked trying to hit the man on top of me with my knees. This had been going on for some ten minutes by this time, I was becoming tired but there was no way I was going to comply with these men. I had an idea of what might happen if I went quiet and weak, what they might do with me, so fighting was the only way out. I thought at that moment – this is how I am going to die, this is where life ends for me at just 12 years of age. I felt sad for a moment but then almost totally resigned to my fate. At that point the man sitting on me got off and released his grip. I jumped up and ran to my mother again who was holding her cut mouth. I saw a trickle of blood running though her fingers and I looked at the soldiers and asked them, 'Why?' At that moment, Mother and I were grabbed and thrown through the doorway into the hall with the others and then the door was shut. The soldier kicked it shut in fury with his boot. We remained inside that hall without any water, sanitation or anywhere comfortable to sleep for a whole night. By morning the place stank of urine: it was horrible. Some hours after first light the door was opened and the few girls who had been separated were pushed in through the door which was then left open. I watched as these girls, crying with fear, ran to the comfort of their mothers. Each had been subjected to rape throughout the night. I know what happened as the girl that I knew, whom I choose not to name here, told me of her ordeal.

She told Ellie:

We were taken into an empty house and the soldiers chose which girl they wanted. After that there was no choice but to go with them as escape was impossible. They had all the exits guarded by an armed soldier. In German language we were told by one of their translators, 'If you refuse to do as we ask you will be shot, and you will not be seeing your mothers again. Do as you are told and you may live.' They weren't really interested in the older women – they wanted the younger ones, virgins preferably, so they could, in a sense, leave their mark upon them for life. These soldiers appeared cold and emotionless and maybe their war had made them that way. Maybe they had families killed by the Germans and this was their revenge, I don't know. The only thing I could do was lie down quietly, take the pain and let them do what they wanted to do with me. All I can say is that it was a humiliating and degrading experience that I would wish on no one. I was forced to do all sorts of things, things that made me feel physically sick and was raped afterwards. They plied us with alcohol which burned our throats, dulled our pain and gave us bad headaches. I was 18 years old at that time, but there were younger girls of 10 and 15 in there, all of whom suffered the same fate as I did. At first light the next morning they put us all together in one of the rooms and threw us our clothing and told us to get out, to go. So, we all walked out and made our way back to the hall from which we had been taken. Our mothers had thought we were all dead, that they had probably killed us after having their fun with us. Our mothers were beside themselves with grief at what they knew had been done to us, but could do nothing but take it as we had no weapons, no means of fighting back and there were far too many of them anyway: we would all have been slaughtered.

Ellie continues:

So, I thought to myself at the time this is how we have to live, to take things day by day and deal with every situation as it unfolds. Each new day I thought to myself: *Will I have to fight again today? Will today be that day I lose my battle with these soldiers and they rape me like they have with so many?* Your mind goes into a kind of survival mode and I know I made a certain peace with myself, that I would rather they kill me than have the pleasure of raping me. It's a state of mind only one in that situation would understand. The thing was, with the Germans, whom most of us didn't want in our country, telling us what to do and what to think and drafting our fathers into their army or Wehrmacht and things like that it was different, it wasn't so bad. Under the Germans there was a clear set of rules and principles that if you followed you would have no problems at all. Under the Russians there were no such rules such as, 'If we do this or if we do that, we will be safe'. When the Russians came, they brought anarchy, a total breakdown of discipline and structure which meant they did as they pleased, and we lived in constant fear of them and what they might do next. Living under those circumstances, which is what we had to endure, was far worse than anything the Nazis had brought with them. That is the best way I can explain this to you: the differences between the Soviets and the Germans were huge. What really hurts me today are these so-called armchair historians who say the rape figures in Vienna were exaggerated. That is a lie, I was there, and I saw with my own eyes the young girls and women they rounded up and took away. I saw them in the days following their ordeals with blackened eyes, scratches and bruises all over their bodies and lumps of hair torn out of their scalps. When you see this time and time again you stop counting the victims. Even today it sends a shiver down my spine when I think how close I came to being violated by them. Even today I am haunted by those dreadful experiences and they will remain with me until I die. You don't just get over these things; it's just not that simple.

Soon it would be the turn of the Austrian cities of Linz and Graz to face the Red Army assault. It would be Red Army soldiers of the 3rd Ukrainian Front that the young Herti, along with her mother and little sister Mädy, would develop such terrifying memories of. Generally, the first wave of Red Army soldiers behaved well as they advanced through Austrian territory. These were the spearhead troops, the professionals who neutralized their enemy and pushed onwards. It was the second wave that were the ruthless, ill-disciplined mobs that looted Austrian properties and raped girls and young women in an orgy of violence and sexual excess that lasted for several weeks.

Meanwhile, as the Soviets were flooding into Austria, in Graz, Herti continued her clandestine listening to the BBC news on the radio, which conflicted significantly with the information still being broadcast by the Nazis. However, there was growing uncertainty about the immediate aftermath of war and the fate of Austrian civilians. As she continues:

The BBC informed me that Hitler was losing, yet the local news still maintained that the German army was progressing and fighting well – more Nazi propaganda was published every day. One item of propaganda designed to instil fear was that if we were to be occupied by Russian troops then all the women would be tortured and raped and all the men shot. Of course, I felt sure this was just more misinformation. Then suddenly, at the end of April 1945, everything on the local news changed. Russian, French, American and British troops were advancing through France, Germany and Poland, nearer and nearer to Austria, reinforcing what I already knew from the BBC World Service. On 8 May, news broke that the war had ended. For the past seven years Austria had been under the control of Germany. Vienna was still a German stronghold and the Russians were determined to gain ground here. I desperately hoped and prayed that the British forces would be the first to reach us – they were approaching from the west of Graz and were about thirty kilometres away. The prospect of being under Russian control was truly terrifying. However, unfortunately, it was the Russian forces that arrived first and laid claim to this region and my concerns were justified. Whereas the Germans had, by and large, been smartly dressed, polite and disciplined, the Russians, comprising Ukrainians and Bulgarians and Cossacks, were a dishevelled and motley assortment of ragged and ill-disciplined men. I remember their scruffy Cossack hats and their long, shabby, threadbare coats hanging loosely around their bodies. No doubt they had experienced dreadful events during the preceding years but, in addition, they came from tough, uncivilized parts of Eastern Europe and Mongolia and they were extremely hard and violent members of the human race. So, the end of the war came with a sense of great anxiety about our future – we were far from settled and very uncertain about our fate and, yet again, we found ourselves living from day to day with stress and worry.

In Vienna, many of the famous and finest buildings were in ruins. There was no electricity, water or gas and there were bands of people looting and plundering property and assaulting and raping civilians in the absence of a police force. The initial Soviet assault forces were focused on their task of defeating the Germans and generally behaved well but the second wave of Soviet troops were responsible for an unbelievable level of violence. My Uncle Rudi, my mother's youngest brother, had a vineyard a short distance from Vienna. I had so many happy memories of visiting his family there – we would sit outside on pleasant, warm evenings with candles alight and Uncle Rudi offering samples of his wines for tasting. Now Vienna was in ruins and the Russians were ransacking every home. Uncle Rudi's village was not spared and I was told that when the Russians came, the villagers were corralled outside where the soldiers held all the men at gunpoint, forced to stand in a row outside their house, while all the young girls were taken and raped. It seems the older women, including my aunty, were spared but the terror of such an event must have been truly dreadful. The men were impotent to protect their loved ones and daughters, and no one knew if they would even be allowed to survive the ordeal. Even when the brutish soldiers left the village the nightmares remained with the inhabitants, probably for the rest of their lives. Wherever the Russians were stationed they brought fear and terror to the communities.

Now these terrible armed Russian troops were occupying Graz and our county of Styria in place of the Germans and it was not long before I had my first encounter with them, learning at first hand just how terrifying they were. I had thought that being controlled by German forces was bad enough but now a new and more frightening force was overseeing our lives. A few days after the end of 'hostilities', the so-called end of the war, I rode my bicycle into Graz, anxious to see what changes had occurred and to find out anything I could about what was actually happening. As I neared the River Mur I stopped as I noticed an open-topped lorry on the opposite side of the road. The back of the lorry was loaded with young girls. I think I recognized one girl as someone I knew whose family owned a lovely hotel in Graz, but I could not be certain, and I never found out what became of her. As I stood watching, one of the Russian guards saw me and began to approach me. Of course, he was armed, and I knew I was easily in range. I did not wait for him to get closer but turned and ran as hard as I could towards the river, having dropped my bike by the roadside. Scrambling into the undergrowth I hid myself and prayed he would not find me. Eventually he gave up looking and returned to the lorry. I waited for several minutes, keeping absolutely still, until I was sure they had driven off before cautiously emerging from my refuge. Naturally, my bicycle had gone and so I was obliged to walk home, furious that I had lost my means of getting around quickly. Despite this loss I was just so thankful for all my physical training and high fitness levels which had enabled me to outrun my potential abductor. I had no idea what was to become of the girls on the lorry but can only surmise their fate, especially in the light of the earlier propaganda predictions and also what was shortly to happen to me. Rumour had it that many truckloads of young women were taken to Russia and further east to be used as sex workers. Many simply disappeared, their destiny unknown. I had certainly had a lucky escape on this occasion.

As I made my way home I thought how excited I had been about the potential changes I would be able to report back to my mother, but now it seemed things were not going to turn out as positively as I had hoped and the feeling of anticipated happiness gradually ebbed away. In addition, the loss of my bicycle would have a big impact on my 'foraging' responsibilities.

The incident in Graz had made me much more cautious and I curtailed my trips out, preferring to stay closer to home where I felt more secure. A few days later, Mother, Mädy and I were back at our house with a friend, Diana, who had recently returned from being evacuated and was helping us to sort through some of our possessions. Diana was an attractive 32-year-old, a good friend and a sensible, mature woman. After busying ourselves during the morning, we had just had lunch and were enjoying a comfortable chat when suddenly the door burst open and three Russian soldiers brandishing rifles charged in and started ransacking the house. They found some items of my father's police uniforms and made the assumption that we were Nazis because of the swastika insignia. I immediately thought of all my medals achieved at school for running and other sports, all of which bore the swastika emblems: I knew then I would have to get rid of them if I only got the chance. As luck would have it, I was wearing an apron with a large pocket on the front so, while the men were occupied in their search for anything of value and Mother was following them around, I quickly grabbed the opportunity to go to my bedroom and slip the medals in the apron pocket. Then I went to the bathroom and flushed them down the toilet, never to be seen again. Our lavatory emptied into a sort of septic tank – a large barrel – and when it was full it would be taken away and emptied by being rolled onto the surrounding fields. I have often wondered if my medals were ever found amongst the harvested vegetables!

It was hard to accept these incredibly foul and uncivilized men in our house, but they had the power and weapons to do as they pleased. One particularly disgusting soldier actually defecated on top of a basket of laundry while another washed his face with the water in the toilet bowl! I had never witnessed such behaviour and it certainly made the propaganda appear much more believable. We were very frightened. Then one of the soldiers made my mother and little sister stand to one side and aimed the rifle at them while the other two took Diana and me at gunpoint out of the house. I was desperate to stay and protect Mother and Mädy – I had made a promise to Father – but what could I do? The soldier guarding them had remained in the house and I was terrified about what might happen to them. How dreadful it must have been, too, for my mother to have to watch helplessly as her daughter was led away. Diana and I were marched across the garden towards the gate and, as we approached it, one of the soldiers suddenly grabbed at my gold earrings and ripped them from my ears – they must have been clip-ons as I do not recall having injured ears – and then snatched the watch from my wrist. The earrings were pretty ones decorated with blue forget-me-nots and the watch was also very lovely. Both had been precious confirmation gifts from my godmother. With the rifle prodding from behind we were frogmarched out of the garden and along the short distance to the local brewery.

This building was a long, barn-like construction with a lower level below ground used for storage and a large, open-plan space on the ground floor used mainly for business purposes, such as meetings and conferences. A staircase led to the upper floor that had been the living accommodation of the owners. Naturally the brewery was not functioning at the time as the owner was away in the German army and the building itself had been requisitioned for occupation by the Russian troops. Once inside Diana and I were vastly outnumbered by these brutes and we realized escape would be impossible. The soldiers who had 'captured' us shouted some words at us which we did not understand, but a Yugoslav worker at the brewery had seen and heard what had happened and he translated for us: 'You will be killed at 6 p.m. today.' Then a hatch was opened, and we were both thrown down a long, steep chute into the cellar where the barrels were stored. I remember noticing it was 2 o'clock when we were thrown in. So, we had four hours before we would be killed. Here it was cold, damp and completely dark. We felt our way around, sat on a couple of barrels and contemplated what the Yugoslav had told us. Diana was inconsolable and could not stop crying. I definitely remember not feeling scared so much as angry about what was happening to us and concern for my mother who would be desperately worried about me. I remember saying to Diana, 'Let's hope that we die quickly – I don't want to have to lie down here in pain for a long time.' But Diana was unable to respond as she was crying too much all the time we were in the cellar. Even had I been able to talk with her, I doubt that we would have had any chance of coming up with a plan – our situation was hopeless and I had the additional worry that I had no idea what they had done to Mother and Mädy. If they had been spared, they would be so anxious about us, not having any idea where we were or what was happening to us.

We stayed in the pitch-black darkness for hours that seemed like an eternity – we had no way to tell how long we were there or if, indeed, the 6 o'clock deadline had arrived. At last the hatch was opened and a shaft of light spilled in. Two of the Russian soldiers came down the stairs next to the chute and made us walk up a few steep steps at gunpoint towards what I expected to be our execution. However, they clearly had alternative plans, at least to pass the time before killing us. They forced us upstairs to the living accommodation situated above the main brewery. One soldier took Diana into one of the bedrooms whilst the other took me into a bedroom across the corridor. For some strange reason he first made me wash his disgusting black and stinking feet – there was a bowl of water and he gave commands which made it clear what I was to do. This in itself would have made me quite sick had I not been even more fearful of what else might be about to happen. I was determined to do all I could to avoid this! He started to undo his trousers and then threw me across the bed. He was filthy and smelled really bad: this was gross, animalistic behaviour and not something I was prepared to give in to. With all the strength I could muster I fought him, kicking hard in his groin and pummelling him with my fists. I continued to kick and punch fast so he could not pin me down. In the background I could hear

Diana screaming and crying, making me even madder and more determined not to give in. Yet again, I was silently appreciative of all the hard physical exercise that had been such a major part of my education under the Nazi regime! Eventually the door opened and the soldier who had been with Diana stood in the doorway and it became apparent he had decided it was time for the two men to swap over. 'My' soldier – whose name was Ivan – got up from the bed and, as they stood talking in Russian, presumably about the swap and my 'non-cooperation', I noticed his rifle had been left on the bed. Without a second thought, I grabbed it and aimed it at the soldiers. They turned, surprise and shock etched on their faces: *Who was this aggressive, feisty, unmanageable teenage girl?* They were immobile for less than a split second, before they launched themselves at me. Truly, I had no idea how a rifle worked so I threw it down and ran for the open window, flinging myself out even though it was from the first floor and I had no idea what was beneath me. As I hit the ground, I knew I had badly hurt my ankle. The ground had been hard and unforgiving. The pain was tremendous, but I knew I had to get up and run. Quickly I glanced around to get my bearings and was horrified to see I was surrounded by a squad of soldiers, all of whom looked as disreputable as the two who had taken Diana and me upstairs. There was no way to escape now. This time I was pushed back into the building and into a huge dining hall containing a large table at which sat all the other soldiers who were billeted here. Diana was there, seated alongside one of the soldiers who had raped her. I was told to sit down on the seat next to her, noticing as I did so that the soldier on my other side was Ivan, the one I had been fighting with just a short while earlier. Placed on the table in front of us were two large glasses of neat vodka. We were ordered to drink them and immediately the glasses were refilled, and we were ordered to drink again. At some point I must have blacked out as the next thing I was aware of was opening my eyes and coming round, with my head on the table, still sitting in the same seat. Now, however, the table was empty and, in fact, the whole room was empty with no soldiers to be seen anywhere. I wondered if perhaps they had assumed I was dead and had decided to leave me there. I staggered to my feet, unstable as a result of the alcohol and also the injury to my ankle. I lurched around the walls of the room making my way to the doorway and then into the entrance hall. Here my luck ran out as several soldiers reappeared. At the bottom of the staircase was a large, thick, upright pillar so I managed to grab hold of it, wrapping my body and arms around it as tightly as possible, locking my fingers together. I could feel more than one soldier pulling me, but I couldn't tell exactly how many men were trying to get me to loosen my grip. I held on for as long as I could but then, miraculously, the front door was thrown open and my mother walked in. Now, a mother protecting her offspring is a formidable sight and these soldiers, caught off-guard like this, in an obviously malicious and wicked act, were so surprised they let go of me. Mother stepped forward with a sense of bravado and a confidence I'm sure she didn't really feel and took hold of my hand. Together we walked out of the door and away from that horrible building. Though my ankle hurt so much, I was determined to walk home and, leaning on mother, we steadily made our way to relative safety. As I limped along, Mother told me Diana had managed to get away and had gone straight to find her to tell her exactly what had happened and where I was. What courage Mother showed when she came barging into the brewery and how grateful I was that she saved me just in time. I was incredibly grateful that, in spite of her own ordeal, Diana had had the presence of mind to go to my mother. From there, I have no idea where she went or what happened to her after that awful experience: I never saw her again.

Now, however, we knew it would only be a matter of time before the soldiers came back to find us so going back to our own home again would not be an option. Collecting my little sister from our house, the three of us set off to walk to a friend's house where we knew we would be welcome and could hide. By now it was after 9 p.m. and the curfew had taken effect, so our journey was even more risky. The safest place to walk was along the ditch of a small brook which took us very near to our friend's house. My ankle was excruciatingly painful, but I had no choice but to walk on it – we just had to keep going. Eventually we arrived and were so glad to get safely inside after what had been an exceptionally gruelling and horrendous day. Even now, all these years later, I look back and remember vividly every moment of that day when I came so close to being raped and when I expected not to survive past 6 o'clock. Yet again, I thanked my lucky stars that I had been spared and could continue on my mission to look after my mother and sister. I had had a truly remarkable escape that day and once more I wondered how on earth I had managed to 'get away with it'.

The war had supposedly ended yet these terrors were somehow infinitely worse than anything we had previously faced, and we had become acutely aware that our ordeal was far from over. I wondered whether my luck would continue to hold out and if I would manage to 'get away with it' in the future.

Indeed, the very next morning there was a loud hammering on the door. Outside were more Russian soldiers, this time demanding entry and on a quest to find items to pillage and young women to rape. Anxious that today I would not be so lucky, Mother insisted that I make my escape and she told me to leave straight away through the back door, across the garden and over the fence. Ignoring the pain in my ankle, I did as she said, fleeing swiftly from the house and taking absolutely nothing with me. I had just a vague plan forming in my mind of getting out of the Russian-occupied area and to where the British were based, feeling sure that only there would I be safe. I left my mother and sister behind, not knowing what would happen to them now but hopeful that they would be safer without me at this time. It did seem that the Russians were only interested in girls of a certain age range so I prayed they would be alright. Sooner or later I would return to take care of them again, I felt sure, though I had no way of knowing just how long I would be away from home.

I have often thought about my mother's amazing bravery and selflessness in sending me away. This was an act of great courage, knowing that I would inevitably face many dangers ahead but conscious that remaining meant almost certain rape and brutality at the hands of these cruel men who had supposedly released us from Nazi tyranny. When Mother and I met again we did not talk about these times and, in fact, over the decades to come we spent many holidays together with opportunities to discuss what happened during that awful period, but we never did. As for so many who had terrible war experiences, we found it safer not to revisit the horrors of our shared past.

It is worth noting here with regard to Herti's reference to the Russian soldier 'Ivan' who tried in vain to violate her that 'Ivan' was used by both Germans and Austrians in the Second World War to describe certain Russian soldiers. Russian soldiers who earned the nickname 'Ivan' due to their brutal, impassive and sexually sadistic conduct, often came from the lower-ranking, ill-disciplined ranks of the Soviet military. These men were usually Cossacks, Mongols or criminals released under the condition that they earn their freedom by fighting in the Red Army, often in penal battalions. Many of these 'Ivans' were dangerously unstable individuals, held in contempt by their fellow Red Army comrades and who should never have been released from imprisonment under any circumstances. It is a reflection on humanity itself that those supposedly liberating the people of Austria were unable (or unwilling) to even attempt to differentiate between those who had supported the Hitler regime and those who had not. Both were treated with equal contempt by the Soviets. How you fared as an

Austrian citizen at that terrible time depended entirely on which side of the Allied occupation you came under.

Amelia 'Milly' Keller recalls a completely different perspective of the end of the war and the liberation of Innsbruck, which occurred on 3 May 1945 when units of the United States 103rd Infantry Division arrived in the city:

We in Innsbruck had been driven into the countryside camps by the heavy bombing of the city. It was there in the early May that word was being put around that an important radio broadcast was to be made by our Gauleiter, Herr Franz Hofer. The people who lived in the farmhouse and who owned the land where we had our camp had informed everyone to gather at the stable yard, as an important announcement was going to be made. So we all got up and walked wearily to the old stable yard to hear this broadcast. The farmer had brought his only radio set and placed it by the window and asked everyone to be silent as the Gauleiter spoke. Herr Hofer informed us that the Americans were not far away and that we should not be frightened and there should be absolute compliance with the American commanders and absolutely no resistance was to be offered. He repeated several times over about not resisting, that anyone hiding any form of a weapon would be in serious trouble if they attempted to use it. Anyone with a weapon was told that now was the right time to dispose of it. Any Hitler Youth members thinking of becoming martyrs for the Nazi cause were also told in no uncertain terms they would be just wasting their time and that they were to stand down immediately. In effect he was telling us the war was now over. When the American forces arrived at our camp the whole area was searched for weapons, including the farmhouse and outbuildings. Most of us just watched in silence as we knew they were suspicious of us all. You were not permitted to talk to them at first, just do as instructed and be polite and helpful to them in their duties. Over the days that followed the arrival of the Americans they brought in German-speaking American soldiers and conversation with them slowly developed. I felt that they were trying to gauge our individual allegiances, to see if we still accepted National Socialist ideas. When my turn came to talk, I was interviewed by a man who introduced himself as Major Paul Ibbott. I admit to being anxious and began babbling to the point where he had to tell me to calm down and speak slowly. I was asked all kinds of questions, such as: Was I a follower of the Hitler regime? Did I feel Hitler was right or wrong? Did I join the Hitler Youth for girls and, if so, did I join willingly? Were my parents supportive of the Nazis? Did I receive any special training for anything? I was eager to answer all of the questions and I also told him about the time I put my mother's sugar supply into the fuel tank of the German truck. He seemed amused by this tale and told me I was very lucky I did not get caught. It felt as if a huge burden had been lifted from my shoulders by answering the questions. The Americans treated us well and gave us food and medical attention. There were a few 'rotten apples' amongst us who were soon rooted out and taken away for questioning. It seemed at this time that there were some Austrians with old scores to settle and those who had collaborated with the Germans were soon picked out. I remember a woman walking around our makeshift camp with two American soldiers. She would stop and look at groups of men then walk on to the next. Suddenly she pointed at one and said, 'There he is – that's him, that one there!' The man was promptly taken away. Whether he was guilty or not was up to the Allied authorities to decide and if he was then I hope he was punished accordingly.

Back in Vienna, Hilde Schubert and her family continued to huddle away inside their damaged home hoping that the marauding Red Army soldiers would bother them no further. Hilde recalls:

Night-time was the worst for us. As we huddled in the pitch blackness of our living room, we were too scared to even light a candle, afraid that somehow it may act as a beacon to passing Russian soldiers who might then come in and violate us again. We remained huddled up behind the old sofa and outside we could hear the drunken singing of Russian soldiers and the sound of glass bottles being smashed as they celebrated their victory. As we sat in silence and darkness my thoughts turned to Father. *Where was he? Was he alive and now a prisoner of war or was he dead?* I dared not share my thoughts with Mother or poor Katrin as both were suffering enough as it was. We couldn't go anywhere as we were too afraid to move and, besides, if Father did come back, he wouldn't know where we had gone if we had left the house. Our sleep over the nights that followed was fitful. It was not so much sleep but 'cat napping', when you fell into a kind of deep sleep then woke after several minutes. It was like that on and off throughout the night. I can recall falling into one such deep sleep yet at the same time being aware of everything and every sound around me. After a few nights of literally no proper sleep you start to sleep in the daytime. One morning we were all fast asleep having not slept properly during the night, when Russian soldiers came in. In an instant we were rigid, sitting up, with that gnawing sense of fear in the pits of our stomachs. To our shock one of them asked us, 'Are you alright? Are any of you in need of medical attention? Have you got any food?' My mother spoke first and told them, '*Nein*', that we hadn't got any food and the only water available was in the outside toilet. This Russian was not like the ones we had encountered earlier and he seemed to have a kind face, one you felt you could trust, and his manner appeared genuine too. He told us, 'You can now come out of there as there is no need to hide any more.' It was then Mother told him that Katrin, her eldest daughter, had been sexually assaulted by four Russians around a week ago. He stood there for a moment deep in contemplation before assuring us, 'No harm will come to you as I am in charge of this area now and my men will not harm you, but I cannot guarantee your safety if you leave this area. Do you understand?' We nodded at him and knew we had little choice other than to trust him and take his word. We sheepishly came out one by one; Mother gathered the little ones and we went outside into the daylight for the first time in over a week. The sunlight felt warm on our faces, yet the light was blinding, and it took several minutes before we could see properly. It was an unexpected scene – there were people we knew walking around picking up things off the ground and standing in groups talking. Our Russian pointed over towards a line of people and told us, 'If you go there and wait in the line there is hot soup and some bread. It is not much, but it will keep you alive.' As we stood in the line we were joined by neighbours, all of whom had stories to tell – some good, others not. My mother was talking with a woman she knew who had a daughter the same age as me who told my mother the Russians had taken her and raped her and that she was powerless to stop them. It seemed every other woman or young girl you spoke to had been raped or knew some poor soul who had. Maybe the Russians that were here now were the good ones but we wondered where the bad ones had gone and if they would ever come back. As Austrian refugees began to return to what was left of our city, they too had stories of murder and rape. These stories continued to circulate among us for around a month or so, if I recall right. Maybe it stopped after that because these ill-disciplined creatures had been told to stop by their commanders. I don't know. It was only later that the Russian officer, whom we called our 'Russian friend', explained that discipline among the Soviet second waves was difficult to maintain as many of these men were illiterate peasants, drunks, thieves, murderers and rapists, some of whom were freed convicts who would be pardoned if they survived. Among these men were

Siberians and Mongolians with their Oriental features – not so much Russians but Asiatic people known throughout history as cruel and brutal. Then there were those men from the Ukraine and southern Russia, predominantly East Slavic-speaking people. These Cossack people were known for being expert horsemen and hunters and were excellent fighting men. Yet again they were ill-disciplined and enjoyed rape – even their own women so what chance did any of ours have if confronted by them? I did a great deal of research on these peoples in the post-Second World War years when we moved away from Vienna. I wanted to try and understand their psychology but even after years of research I couldn't fathom them out, what made these people tick, what made them so savage. It was a professor of anthropology at the university at Duisburg in Essen who told me years later that they behave in a primitive manner: 'Because they are born and live in a harsh and primitive world. If they want food, they simply go out and kill it. Sometimes they will spend days searching for food, sometimes in conditions unbearable to us westerners. If these men want a woman, there is no seduction, no fine meal and wine, no mating ritual – just brute force. They take women against their will, if need be. That is how these people live and exist, and to them this way of life, despite being hard, is perfectly normal to them. Under normal circumstances you would have been totally unlikely to have come into contact with the men of these distant Asiatic cultures. Sadly, it was the war that brought them to you.' I asked the professor, 'So these Asiatics were, in a sense, Stalin's Praetorian Guard?' To which he laughed and replied, 'Well, I wouldn't say Praetorian Guard exactly: that refers to something more elite with a degree of finesse and intelligence. I would say they were more the dogs on the leash at the Praetorians' heels if this makes sense.' It was a miracle that Katrin had not been made pregnant through her rape ordeal when the four men raped her. I don't know how she would have dealt with that. It makes me happy that she did not let them destroy her life though. She did what she did to protect us and all through our later lives I never forgot that. If it hadn't been for Katrin those soldiers would have raped me, my mother and probably the little ones too.

Sadly, our father did not return home from his war. It is the one thing I cannot bear to talk about or mention, even to you. I just can't talk about him and would rather leave it at that as it causes me immense grief even now, all these years later. Yes, it hurts so much it gives me a pain in my stomach. At the war's end we remained in Vienna hoping Father would return and that those dreadful Russians would leave. The Russians it seemed were happy to occupy our city which, under Allied control, became a confusing political and occupational conundrum for me. We knew the Russians would not be leaving their sector of influence in Vienna anytime soon. Despite the kindness shown towards us by some of them, I still harboured much hatred for them. I could never forget what they did to my sister and I felt it was a duty even in the post-war occupation to resist them wherever I could.

As a student in the post-war years I mixed with other teenage girls and boys and we often got together to discuss politics and the future of Vienna. These meetings were strictly covert and kept between students we knew we could trust. We would meet up at one another's homes where we would each contribute to the conversation. For example, if one of us witnessed the Russians arresting an Austrian citizen, we would try to find out why this had happened. This information was collated and then secretly passed on to a contact in Salzburg. We recorded all sorts of activity – if we saw soldiers in any particular place, we wrote it all down and if we saw aircraft active in certain areas we wrote down where and when, types of aircraft and so on. We knew the western Allies had people who were interested in this kind of information, so we did our best to get it for them. It was our way of getting back at the Russians. One of our group even located a military scrapheap.

He found partially burnt documents and a piece of an aircraft control, so he took this and as many of the document remnants he could cram into his pockets to forward to the Salzburg contact, the Russians completely unaware of what we were doing. We were just doing our best to inform on Soviet activity in our city. The other Allied powers were aware of what was going on and kept an eye on everything the Russians did, and we felt we were, if only in a tiny way, helping them. It was still resistance no matter how small it may have been. Years later we often went to stay in Essen where we had a large group of relatives. There Katrin met and married her husband, Bernd, and they had four beautiful children. I married a little late, at the age of 26, and I have three grown-up children with children of their own now.

The Russian occupation of our country ended after ten long years, in 1955. They left the city bankrupt and struggling. I vividly remember the day they started to pull out of Vienna. They gathered everything onto convoys of military vehicles and off they went. As they drove past, they looked at us with that same impassive expression we had endured for many years. I remember one young woman running alongside a vehicle loaded with Russian troops. She was waving a handkerchief at one of the soldiers and wailing, 'Come back! Don't leave me here, don't go!' She appeared beside herself with grief. As the vehicle drove on, she fell to her knees and sobbed her heart out. Nobody went to console her; people just walked on by. One woman spat on her. These women were viewed with contempt by some, like traitors or something. For the majority of us it was just a huge relief when the Russians finally left, and we became independent again. Apart from the years of war, my life has largely been a happy one. We had to rebuild our lives from nothing, but we Austrian people are tough, we didn't just roll over and die – we persevered and, with God's help, we succeeded. It has taken all these years for me to be able to talk about it. I want the world to know all about it and although talking about it opens up many old wounds, I am happy to have finally told my own story of what happened during my war in Austria. All that pain, all that destruction and death, was caused by just one maniac politician. If I blame anyone, I blame him – Austria's most infamous son.

Chapter 9

Getting Away

Having been encouraged to flee her home by her mother, who was fearful for her eldest daughter's safety, Herti made her escape as Red Army soldiers banged on the front door of her house. She recalls:

At least it was daytime and summer, so the days were long and warm, and I did not have to worry about the fact I had no extra clothes with me. I was wearing a summer skirt and blouse with sandals on my feet and, though I did not know it at the time, I would have no other clothing for several months. I was constantly aware of the possibility of being caught and I knew that after curfew I would be at very serious risk. In addition, I had no food or money so all my resourcefulness skills would be put to the test. I could not afford to think about the dreadful pain in my ankle – there was simply nothing to be done about that. I limped on, ignoring the agonizing spasms and focused on keeping my eyes on the way ahead and my senses alert – at all costs I must avoid any confrontation with the Russian soldiers who were patrolling the area so I chose to make my way along tracks that kept me away from the main road. I tried not to think too much about Mother and Mädy and to focus on what I now needed to do. I knew I must stay strong – I had had plenty of practice in being independent and finding ways to survive but this time I was completely on my own, with no way back, no home to go to and no family to give me comfort, no mother to turn to for advice. I made my way, hobbling as best I could, over the four miles to the railway station, where I had previously foraged in the goods trucks. I tried not to think about the dead bodies I had tripped over on that occasion. I believed that my only chance of escape was to somehow board a train to get near the border of the Russian-occupied area and from there to make my way across the mountains and thus reach British-occupied territory where I would be safe. I tried hard to look inconspicuous at the station – I think my skills at deception and quick thinking had developed quite effectively over the past couple of years. However, there was no security here and absolutely no one working in an official capacity. Without station staff, people could simply make their way onto the platform and wait hopefully for a train. On the platform I noticed two other girls who, like me, appeared to be looking around cautiously and I guessed they might also be trying to escape the same fate. We began a conversation and it was quickly apparent that I was correct in my assumption. Helen and Christine were desperate to get away from the potential fate they might be subjected to by the Russians. We decided that we would stay together on the train and make the journey across the mountains together, thus providing each other with company and moral support as well as the knowledge we would stand a better chance if we were a team. Our biggest problem, however, was that we had no identity documents or ration cards – in fact, nothing to prove our nationality. But we would have to try, anyway, and hope that we would eventually reach our destination and be met with sympathy and support. As we three waited on the otherwise deserted platform we got to know each other a little more, discovering our respective stories. Christine, a well-educated grammar school student aged 17, hoped to become a chemist. She was clearly very intelligent and ambitious for her future career. Helen, on the other hand, was older – in her mid- to late-twenties – and was a relatively poor girl who lived and worked on a farm. Though both girls were terrified about what they might suffer at the hands of the Russians, it was the Germans who had punished Helen severely after she had been found to have assisted British servicemen: an airman had parachuted in and landed on Helen's parents' farm where he had been offered shelter by them. The Gestapo discovered the airman and one way they had punished the family was to shave off all Helen's hair – during the time we were together Helen wore a scarf tied firmly over her bare head. I have no idea what fate befell her parents – I don't think we talked about such things. Yet again I realized just how lucky I had been in not being caught.

Eventually, a small train pulled into the station and we managed to squeeze on board as it was packed with no seats available. We stood in the corridor beside one of the French officers who was accompanying a sizeable group of French people crammed onto the train. As usual, I took advantage of the opportunity during the one-hour journey to Voitsberg to start a conversation with the officer and try to gain any relevant information that might help us. Apparently, he had permission to take up to 250 French workers across the border and back to France. We told him of our situation, and he said he would help us. We would need to pretend we were part of the French group and hope not to be challenged, but if we were, he would deny all knowledge and we would be on our own. It was a risky scheme but our best chance, so we swiftly agreed.

On arrival at Voitsberg, which was at the extremity of the Russian-occupied zone, we disembarked together with the group of French workers. I am sure that Helen and Christine both felt every bit as anxious as I did but we made every effort to blend in with the group making our way, as directed, towards an orchard where we were to await further orders. It was an extremely hot day and time passed slowly: we knew that if we were caught trying to cross without papers we would be in serious trouble and the increasing heat of the midday sun during our lengthy wait did not help one bit. I had had nothing to eat since my small breakfast hours ago and there was no water available either. Eventually, after more than two hours, we were called forward and told it was time to queue up to cross the border out of Soviet territory. We were instructed to form a line, two abreast, so the Russian guards could select individuals at random for spot checks. I watched anxiously as a number in front of us were told to show their documents which appeared to be in order.

We three girls separated and placed ourselves amongst the group as inconspicuously as possible. Helen was nearer to the front; I was somewhere in the middle and Christine towards the rear. Just as the guards reached the point where Helen was standing, they selected some more people to produce their documents but fortunately Helen was not one of them. As the guards made their way slowly down the line towards me, carefully scrutinizing everyone, a Russian soldier pointed at the woman right in front of me. I heard her say something that sounded like '*Frantsuzskiy*' which appeared to confirm her nationality as French to the Russian and he moved on to me. Now it was my turn to prove my identity. With nothing to show I took a chance and copied the previous woman's utterance of '*Frantsuzskiy*' and, miraculously, it worked, and he moved on to the people behind me. Turning around, I watched as the guards approached Christine, holding my breath. Luckily the whole group appeared to be 'in order' and at last the barrier was raised allowing us to move out of the holding area without incident and thus everyone arrived safely across the border, out of the Russian-occupied zone and into 'no-man's land'. This, now, was a place of relatively safety but our journey was far from over. We expressed our huge gratitude to the French officer who had helped us get there as they went on their way and we prepared for the next stage of our arduous travels.

We had not thought very much about what we would do after getting across the border so we sat for a while in the ditch at the roadside (there was no verge) to allow ourselves a little time to reflect on our good fortune so far and to allow the fear and tension of the recent past to gradually ebb away. Plus by now my ankle was excruciatingly painful and I had no idea how I would manage to walk any further on it – an issue that became more apparent as we turned our thoughts to the future: we knew we had to get to the end of 'no-man's land' – an area that extended for approximately eight kilometres – and then face the challenge of being admitted to the British sector, again with no documents to identify us. We realized that our only hope was to obtain a lift but, if this was not possible, we would somehow simply have to walk over the mountains and try to enter the British zone unnoticed. At this moment, however, we were simply happy to sit in the warmth of the late summer afternoon and relax for a while – truly a welcome treat after our gruelling day.

After a while we heard a vehicle approaching and, looking along the road, we saw a truck travelling in the direction we needed to go. It was too good an opportunity to miss so I jumped up and stood in the road waving furiously for the driver to stop. When the truck came to a halt I ran to his door and called out, asking if he would be willing to give the three of us a lift across no-man's land to the British-occupied zone. Once more we had struck lucky and the driver agreed to take us, so up we jumped into the back of his open truck. Here we found ourselves sitting on top of a very significant load of rifles – this was an Austrian partisan pickup truck delivering a supply of arms! We sat on the weapons for the duration of the eight-kilometre journey, thinking that it was all very well having a gun at your disposal if you knew how to use it. There had been times, indeed, just very recently, when I would have done so had I only known how to shoot!

Arriving at the border our driver slowed down and then stopped to allow us to get down from the back of the truck. There were two soldiers at the border post who I discovered were Irish

Fusiliers. As anticipated, they requested our documents and we admitted we had none. We were considerably dismayed to learn that without documentation we would not be allowed to pass into the British sector. Even if we had ID, without ration cards we would not be admitted as food was scarce even for those entitled to it. We had no 'Plan B' and were truly stumped as to what we could possibly do next. Early evening was upon us and, although the summer's days were long and there was still plenty of light, we would need some shelter and could not manage without food for too much longer. Fortunately, however, the guards took pity on us, accepting our stories and realizing that we were 'genuine', having escaped with just what we stood up in. They allowed us through and into Koflach in the Carintia region, now under British occupation, but warned us that without ration cards it would be practically impossible to get any food. They suggested that we would need to travel further into the country where there was a possibility of obtaining some food in exchange for work, thus improving our chances of survival. There was a chance that if we made our way to the centre of the small town of Koflach, we could approach the British battalion that had temporarily established their base at the school where we would be best placed to secure help with onward transport.

We walked the short distance to the middle of town and arrived at the school, as directed, noticing an increasing number of lorries as we got nearer. These vehicles were fully loaded and appeared ready to travel in convoy. This was yet another opportunity too good to miss so I approached one of the lorry drivers, who happened to be an Australian, and asked him where they were going and if it would be possible for us to have a ride with them, if it meant we would get closer to a more helpful destination. He explained to me that the convoy was on its way to a village called Priel on the outskirts of Wolfsberg, to a large POW camp, Stalag XVIII-A. Just one week earlier, prior to the end of the war, this camp had been used to house up to 7,000 British POWs and it was now to be run as a detention centre by the British troops. Fortunately, the Australian sergeant agreed that we could travel with them and, in fact, there was plenty of space for all of us in the cab, so we climbed on board into the relative comfort of the cab when compared with our previous transport! Shortly afterwards the convoy set off on its journey to Wolfsberg.

During the journey we talked about our escape from the Russian zone and once more, I was delighted to be able to practise my English language conversation skills. I explained that my ultimate aim was to get to England where I felt sure life would offer me great opportunities! I remember that we did not talk about our 'experiences' of the past – just our hopes and plans for the future. Our driver was both kind and sympathetic and we were immensely grateful to have the help of someone so trustworthy. When we arrived at Wolfsberg he dropped us off at the hospital, thinking that this would be the best place for us to receive the practical help of food and shelter that we now so urgently needed.

The three of us entered the main hospital entrance and explained to the staff there that we had nowhere to go and no food – we were truly refugees and desperately in need of help. After a brief discussion we were offered the use of the hospital basement which had been used as an air-raid shelter, as temporary accommodation, but they were unable to give us any food. Down in the basement there were some beds with straw mattresses and, as we were all so very tired after our difficult day, we were more than happy to lie down and get some rest in safety. Tiredness overcame hunger and we slept soundly.

The following morning the Australian sergeant who had given us a lift the previous day came to the hospital to find us and see how we had managed overnight. Once again, we were struck by his kindness and consideration towards us. He also asked whether any of us could cook! By this time, we three girls had established that, as Christine and Helen were either not very confident or not very skilled in English, I was to be the spokesperson for all of us while they remained silent. This enquiry from our friendly Australian was, indeed, a further stroke of good fortune and, although I had no idea about English 'cuisine' and assumed the others had not either, I quickly said that we were all competent cooks, though might need some guidance about their specific dietary needs! Our wonderful helper told us this would not be a problem and invited us to start work straight away as cooks for the British officers' mess. The most amazing thing about this piece of luck was that we would have access to food ourselves. So off we set with our Australian sergeant, accompanying him to the POW camp where the company was stationed, and there we were shown the kitchens. We were expected to start work the following morning at 6 a.m. Grateful for this life-saving chance, we made our way back to the hospital in good spirits. During the half-hour walk we chatted about our good fortune in finding a place to sleep and somewhere to work that would also provide us with food. Although there had been no mention of payment, we were just happy to know that our most immediate problems had been solved so quickly. I wished, however, that I could somehow let Mother know that I had successfully managed to reach the British zone and not an hour passed when I did not think about her and Mädy, hoping they, too, were safe.

Once back at the hospital, we made our way down to the basement. The room, although large, was extremely basic with no facilities apart from a toilet and a small washbasin. The straw mattresses on our beds were horrible – spikey, rough and lumpy and covered with grubby hessian. We had no idea who had used them before or, indeed, what might be living inside them now! It was high summer and hot and stuffy in the basement: we awoke in the mornings feeling itchy and unclean. We had no sheets, blankets or pillows but these were not such high priorities as food and shelter. Over the coming weeks and months, we did our best to keep as clean as possible but apart from rinsing our underwear at night we were obliged to put on the same clothes each day. However, above all, we were safe so, overall, felt very grateful for our current situation.

As day dawned the following morning we were up and ready to walk to the camp so we would be there in plenty of time for our 6 a.m. start. Though my ankle was still extremely painful, I simply had to put up with it – on balance this injury was a minor issue and there were more important matters to deal with. On arrival, our first task was to light the range cooker so that it would be hot enough for cooking during the day whenever required. As cooks to the officers, we had use of a small kitchen that was adjacent to the dining room used by the twenty-four officers for whom we were to cater. At the end of a very long corridor was an enormous kitchen where the cooking was done for the rest of the troops and where the vast storeroom was situated. Each morning I would visit the main kitchen store to collect all the ingredients needed for the officers' food for the day. There I was able to ask the army cooks for suggestions and advice about what we should cook for each of the three main meals every day. Fortunately, the cooks were happy to help us and I was extremely grateful for their input into the menus we produced. However, no matter how well intentioned we were, our efforts were very much 'trial and error' as none of us really had much idea about cooking – certainly a lot less than I had led the Australian sergeant to believe! But we were all quick learners and soon familiarized ourselves with the preferences of the officers who seemed to be very sympathetic and understanding and, on the whole, satisfied with our attempts.

One of the perks of working in the kitchen was that, at last, we were well fed ourselves which was a great relief. However, it was boiling hot in the kitchen with the range fired up and it was also mid-summer so there was no relief from the stifling heat. With our seriously limited washing facilities we must not have been the 'freshest' of kitchen workers, but we did our best to be as hygienic as possible. Towards the end of summer and as soon as I knew the Russians had left Graz, I managed to get in touch with Mother to let her know where I was and what had been happening to me. Eventually I was able to send some food parcels to her from the camp kitchen supplies. On one occasion I hitchhiked back to Graz to visit her and Mädy and take some extra rations. It meant a great deal to me to be able to carry on supporting Mother and Mädy in this way.

An incident occurred in the middle of one particular day that upset the daily routine that had become established. It was yet another hot summer's day when, as usual, we were working with all the doors wide open to allow as much ventilation as possible. Suddenly a soldier came rushing into the kitchen brandishing a pistol. Helen was standing in front of a huge pot of mashed potatoes that she had been preparing and into this great bowl the soldier threw his sidearm! He then ran through our kitchen and down the long corridor that led to the main kitchen, as two military policemen rushed through the doorway in hot pursuit. I plunged my hand into the bowl of steaming potatoes and pulled out the gun which I handed to one of the policemen. After this little drama, I cleaned out the grubby bits in the dish of potatoes and everything settled down – but we did not tell the officers that they very nearly had a handgun served with their lunch!

After we had been working in the kitchen for about three months, returning each evening to our basic accommodation in the hospital, we were able to find an unfurnished room in the town. We said our goodbyes to the hospital staff, thanked them for helping us in our hour of need and, with cheerful spirits, we took ourselves to our new home. Although we still did not have any proper washing facilities and no beds, it was still a nicer place to stay than the basement of the hospital, being on the first floor of an apartment building with windows and a much more airy and open feeling. Another bonus was that we did not have such a long walk to work each day. Outside there was a courtyard and a large wooden gate that led onto the street. At the main door was a bell that served the whole building, though I do not recall any other people living there while we were there.

However, all things at this time were in a state of flux and nothing stayed the same for long. At the beginning of July, we learned that the camp was to be dispersed and the company was going to be moved to another town in Styria. This meant we would lose our jobs as cooks and again be without food. However, on our last day working at the camp we were given a large sack of food to take back to our accommodation to tide us over. Yet again, we were grateful to the British for their thoughtfulness and kindness, so different from the Russians.

The company was preparing for the move and we were sitting on the floor in our room (we had no furniture at all!) wondering what to do next and thinking of various schemes whereby we could fend for ourselves once again. Suddenly we heard the clanging of the doorbell down below, so I rushed down the stairs to investigate. I crossed the courtyard to the huge outer gate only to discover a British soldier standing there who told me he had heard that there were English speakers in the house. I confirmed that yes, indeed, Christine and I were both competent with the English language. The soldier explained that the company was looking for interpreters to travel with them to their next destination. Once again, good fortune seemed to be with us! With great excitement, I rushed upstairs to tell Christine about this amazing possibility of an interpreter's job with the same company. However, with her usual reticence, Christine decided she did not feel capable of doing the work and declined the offer. I knew that here was a chance for me and I could not afford to let it slip by. It would mean going it alone and leaving my friends behind. I rushed back down the stairs to tell the soldier I would be pleased to take up the offer and he told me to be ready to leave in two hours' time: I was to report to the Commanding Officer with whom I would be travelling. I am sure that Christine and Helen would have continued to support each other but as we said our farewells none of us knew when or if we would meet again. In fact, we never did and, sadly, I have no idea what happened to either of them from that day on.

A short while later I was sitting in the officer's car at the head of the company convoy. I was excited about embarking on this next stage and incredibly grateful that I had this opportunity. I knew as long as I was with the British forces, I would be safe and taken care of. It did not matter that I received no pay – it was enough to have 'board and lodging', to feel I had a 'proper job' and was making a valuable contribution and I was feeling optimistic about the direction of my future pathway. However, I was also wondering just how I would stand the journey as I had developed a fever and a very sore throat which I had not dared disclose for fear of being left behind. I sat back and closed my eyes – all I wanted to do was sleep. But there was work to be done and I was expected to take notes dictated by the CO, Major Cole, throughout the journey. My throat felt swollen and constricted and the pain was dreadful. I could hardly focus on the page in front of me and I began to feel quite sick. Nevertheless, it was imperative that I stay strong and prove myself competent so, somehow, I managed and eventually we arrived at our destination.

Chapter 10

Working Towards My Future

Having been given the opportunity of work and the possibility of a more secure future, it was a remarkable bit of bad luck that Herti should arrive in Judenburg feeling so poorly. Nevertheless, she did her best to carry out the orders she was given, translating for the British officers. She continues her story:

Arriving at the outskirts of Judenburg we separated from the rest of the convoy. The car pulled up in front of a very beautiful villa and I was instructed by Major Cole to inform the occupants that the house was to be requisitioned for occupation by the British forces. Feeling dreadful – both physically and about the task I had been given – I approached the front door and knocked. The door was opened by the owner who greeted me politely but was visibly shocked when I informed him, as instructed, that his family had to pack up and leave the property immediately. I discovered later that this man was a doctor, but I imagine that the news I brought overshadowed any observation he might have made about the sickly looking young woman who delivered this devastating message. In any case, though the family pleaded with me to let them remain in their home, this was to no avail as the officer was adamant that the British officers would be moving into the villa straight away. At last they realized there was no option but to leave and they gathered together a few belongings and left as instructed. We had no idea where they would be going, and they were offered no assistance in relocating. An elderly Portuguese couple who were employed by the doctor's family were asked to remain in the house to carry on with their duties as handyman and housekeeper. I felt so sorry for the family as the door closed behind them and they walked away – this was a horrible task and made me realize that my work as an interpreter would involve other such unpleasant jobs: I would simply have to comply with the decisions of others and the orders I was given. It was particularly nasty having to give instructions to fellow Austrians on behalf of the 'occupying forces' of our country – I felt a certain sense of betrayal towards this family but had to rationalize this action as being the price to be paid for achieving peace.

The house itself was spacious and offered excellent accommodation for the officers billeted there. Outside was a very beautiful garden; downstairs there was accommodation for me, the batman and the Portuguese couple as well as a kitchen, sitting room and dining room. Upstairs were the bedrooms used by the officers – Major Cole and Major Trevor. As soon as we had established ourselves and the rooms had been allocated, I took the opportunity to collapse onto my bed as, by now, I was feeling very poorly. The Portuguese housekeeper came into my room after a while and noticed immediately that I was seriously unwell. She called the batman and another soldier, a 'medic', who checked me over and decided on the basis of my very high temperature that I probably had malaria. He discussed my condition with the officers who considered the best option was to give me quinine tablets. Somehow, in spite of my swollen and painful throat, I managed to swallow them. I know I could hardly speak. I spent a terrible night and, in the morning, it was apparent to everybody that I was desperately in need of proper medical attention so an ambulance was sent for by the housekeeper. The attending paramedic diagnosed diphtheria and I was taken to the local hospital.

On arrival at the hospital I was allocated a bed in a general ward consisting of about fourteen occupied beds. A little while later a doctor came into the ward to check me over. When the nurse indicated where I was, he raised his arm and pointed at me from the end of the ward and shouted loudly, 'Who put this patient in here? She should be in the isolation building!' With that, all the other patients quickly covered their heads with their sheets and blankets to avoid contamination. I was too ill to care much but it was hugely embarrassing, and I felt very guilty that I might have passed on a contagious disease. A nurse approached and told me I would need to move so I was to get up and out of bed. From here I had to walk out of the ward, downstairs to the ground floor and across the hospital grounds to the isolation building. I did not know how I would manage to do this as I felt so very ill. Once I arrived at the reception area, I noticed a nun sitting behind a desk and then I was aware only of the expanse of black and white chequered marble floor as I collapsed and passed out.

Apparently, I was unconscious for four days. As I slowly regained my senses, I noticed a man standing at the foot of my bed who kept asking me who I was. Over and over he repeated his question until eventually I was able to give him my name and a few more details. When he left, I managed to look around me, taking in my surroundings. I noticed a very young child, aged about 2, in the bed next to me who seemed extremely undernourished, thin and very ill. The sound of breathing was heavy, noisy and erratic. As night drew on, I lay listening to the irregular rhythm of each breath. At some point in the night I realized that the breathing had stopped so I used all my strength to call for the nurse. A nun came and discovered that the small child had, indeed, died. She pulled the sheet up over the child and fetched a tall candle which she lit and placed at the foot of the bed. I was left for the remainder of the night knowing that the poor child in the bed next to me was dead. I felt alone, disturbed and traumatized by this sad event.

The following day I received the unbelievably wonderful news that Mother was downstairs! I imagine that once the hospital staff knew who I was, they were able to make contact with my mother who made every effort to get to my bedside, having been informed just how ill I was. Or maybe the British officers had managed to get in touch with her. Anyway, though she had made the journey by hitchhiking all the way she was not allowed to come to my bedside and make direct contact with me because of the infectious nature of my illness. So, I gathered my strength and managed to go to the window on the first floor from where I could lean out and talk to her in the grounds below. She told me about her journey and the lifts she had been given from Graz to Judenburg and I gave her some information about what I had been doing in Wolfsberg and my current job, which I hoped would still be there for me when I was better. I was so fortunate to have this employment with the security that went with it – this was indeed a golden opportunity and therefore I needed to stay there in Judenburg rather than go home to Graz with Mother, where future work prospects were not promising. I was overjoyed that Mother had brought clothes for me from home – at last I could have a change from my now very worn-out skirt and blouse! She was not able to stay any longer with me, however, as she had left Mädy back in Graz with friends so, seeing I was on the road to recovery, she was obliged to make the return journey hitchhiking back home. The pleasure of being briefly reunited with Mother helped me enormously and I did make good progress from this point on. Many years later during one of Mädy's visits with me in England, I found out that my dear little sister had cried the whole time Mother had been away, frightened that she would not make it back and Mädy would be left all alone.

Three days after Mother's visit I was discharged from hospital. I was told to obtain further treatment from my own doctor, to take it easy and that I would need to convalesce and carry on with my recuperation for some considerable time. Not having access to a family doctor and without anyone to look after me, it was impossible to comply with these instructions. My priority was to get back to work as an interpreter as quickly as possible so I walked out of the hospital building and made my way straight to the office where I would be working. On arrival I was told that while I had been in hospital the officers had arranged for me to stay at a hotel in the centre of the town rather than return to the villa. This hotel was just a short distance from the office so was much more convenient and I made my way there at the end of the working day. I had a nice room: I found it very peaceful and was able to get plenty of much-needed rest. I remained lodging in the hotel for a short while before accommodation was provided for me at another villa conveniently situated on the outskirts of town, and from where I could be picked up and taken to work each day and dropped back home in the evening by military transport.

The office consisted of two rooms, one for the two officers to whom I reported – Major Trevor and Captain Dabbs. The second office at the front of the building was occupied by a sergeant and two of his assistants. My main responsibility was to translate the documents that pertained to the Displaced Persons centre which was situated just outside Judenburg. This establishment, like so many others, had been a POW camp but now held many people of various nationalities – Latvian, Polish, Italian, for example – who were awaiting processing before being repatriated. Needless to say, there was a great deal of administration to be carried out and people with no documentation had somehow to have their identity proved before they could be moved on, hopefully to return to their home country and their loved ones. In addition to translation work with Displaced Persons, my language skills were put to use in many other ways. I was sent each morning to help purchase supplies from the bakery and the butcher and any other food provisions required by the camp. Basically, I was on call seven days a week whenever translation from German to English was needed.

Then the happy day came after a few weeks when I heard that Captain Dabbs and his unit were to be transferred to Graz for the opening of a new Displaced Persons facility and I was asked to accompany him and continue my work as his interpreter. I was overjoyed to be going home where I would be reunited with my family. We travelled to Graz in a small convoy. I was sitting in the back of the staff car with Captain Dabbs; his batman and driver were in the front. As we drove Captain Dabbs dictated notes for me and I remember having to overcome the awful feeling of carsickness. Still, it was wonderful knowing I was returning to my hometown now that the Russians had left and to be a part of the British troop contingent who were now going to occupy the whole of Styria and this happy thought sustained me.

Once we arrived, Captain Dabbs and his company set about converting a large grammar school into the new Displaced Persons shelter which was to house some of the few Jewish survivors of the terrible concentration camps. Work was carried out very quickly and the conversion was soon completed. Soon after, a very small group of Jewish people – about half a dozen – were moved into the shelter where they received food and basic medical care before being moved to more permanent accommodation. I believe these people were probably originally from Graz and were in the process of 'coming home', although they would have lost all their possessions and would be starting to rebuild their lives from absolutely nothing. There were many more Jewish people who had lived in Vienna and I imagine the 'DP' facilities there would have dealt with much greater numbers of concentration camp survivors. For me, this was the first time I had come face to face with such survivors and words cannot describe how horrified I felt to witness these poor souls, so emaciated they were little more than skeletons. I have no idea how they had managed to survive, some being barely able to walk without aid, desperately sick and malnourished. However, with the physical and medical help given to them at the DP shelter, they gradually became a little stronger and, with the assistance of the British bureaucracy, many were able to be relocated quite quickly.

Following the successful establishment of the DP facility at Graz, another one was soon constructed at the nearby village of Kapfenberg by Major Cole, who requested that Captain Dabbs and his company should be transferred from Graz to assist in his task there. Again, we were on the move and this time I was working for both Captain Dabbs and Major Cole. The whole company was billeted about four miles away in an old castle called Schloss Graschnitz. The work was very demanding with ever-increasing numbers of people to process which required detailed questioning and corroboration of facts to establish true identities and nationalities. With the increase in the workload, it became apparent that we needed more help with translation, and I was able to recommend my friend, Ditta, who lived in Graz, as an additional interpreter. Ditta had been very ill with TB during the whole of the Russian occupation and had been in hospital in the mountains. In one sense this was very lucky for her because it meant she had escaped the threat of abuse from the terrifying Soviet forces. She was now fully recovered and delighted to have the opportunity to have employment and, like me, to use her English language skills. Ditta moved into the castle with me and we shared a room. What a delight it was to be living in such a beautiful place and to be able to walk in the lovely grounds chatting about ordinary things and to feel that life was getting better every day. I remember there was a large and imposing ballroom in the castle with a piano and I was thrilled to be able to play again – it had been so long since I had played my beloved piano at home. As I played, Ditta and I would enjoy singing together in the ballroom when we had time off from our work. And, of course, we took advantage of the magnificent ballroom to dance with abandon!

Another wonderful memory I have of our time at the castle was of horse-riding in the extensive grounds. I had started riding when I was a very small girl – my grandparents at Laxenburg had horses – so I was a competent rider. I was never afraid on horseback and I do not recall ever falling off, in spite of going as fast I could! Amazingly, the retreating German Army who had occupied the castle had left these lovely animals behind, so it was our good fortune that they were still there when the British took over. Several British officers also took advantage of the opportunity to ride and we had great fun galloping together, forgetting any present worries and obliterating the memories of the past. Such activities made us feel that truly there was a good life ahead and that the horrors of war were finally behind us. This was a fantastic place to live and we enjoyed our time at the castle enormously. One soldier who was a brilliant rider was Sergeant Bill Jones. I had met him previously when I was with Christine and Helen and we were cooking in Wolfsberg. I remember thinking how dashing and handsome he was and after our first meeting I prayed I would have the chance to see him again! Of course, it was just a 'schoolgirl crush' on my part – after all I was 16 and he was 32 and I had no idea if he had a wife and family at home. Though we were both working in the same general area, our paths did not cross again until we were all billeted at the castle. I was so excited to have the chance to spend more time with him. Galloping through the castle grounds with Bill was exhilirating. He was a kind and good friend and, on one occasion, he actually gave me a kiss on the cheek, adding to the 'fairy-tale romance' of our stay at Schloss Graschnitz.

Every morning the officers, Ditta and I would travel in the officers' staff car the short distance to the Displaced Persons facility. Prior to any new arrivals at the camp it was necessary to create the infrastructure required, which included constructing a kitchen and a small medical centre to provide the basic level of care that would be necessary before these people were able to move on, hopefully to their homes. When the camp was up and running we processed the people coming through as swiftly as possible and this camp remained in operation for approximately a year, after which the company was moved to another existing Displaced Persons facility in the small town of Trofaiach, back near Judenburg. Although we were sad to leave the castle, both Ditta and I joined the company there in Trofaiach and continued to work as interpreters for several more months. By now the war had been over for more than two years and I was 18 years old.

However, there were continuing challenges that faced everyone working with the refugees and displaced persons, not least being the constant threat of disease. Most people passing through the camp were in poor health anyway so had little resistance and sickness travelled quickly through the population. Whilst in Trofaiach, a number of people contracted typhoid and typhus, both very infectious. Occasionally it was necessary to transfer very sick people to hospital and I was required to accompany them as their interpreter, along with the medics. Consequently, to protect me from catching any of these diseases I received a whole barrage of inoculations and vaccinations. Though I did not enjoy so many needles being stuck in me I was grateful for the security these injections gave me, thus enabling me to fulfil my supportive role with these sick people both compassionately and effectively. I felt so sorry for the very sick individuals who were gravely ill yet had to endure being transported in the back of large army lorries. Indeed, some did not survive the journey and of those who arrived at hospital still alive many were to die there.

During the early part of 1947 it was apparent that most of our work here was done. Gradually the camp 'residents' had been returned to their homelands and the camp itself had become redundant so was scheduled for closure. As we were no longer required in Trofaiach, I returned to Graz to work with Captain

Dabbs who had now transferred to the Special Investigation Branch along with Captain Galliford. Now I was able to live at home with my family in Graz which made me very happy.

Captain Dabbs's new job meant a huge change for me in my interpreting role, which now became far more complex and demanding. Now I was responsible for translating many complicated documents which often included forensic evidence that was to be used to support prosecutions for war crimes, fatal accidents and rape allegations. These cases were extremely sensitive, and I felt a huge burden of responsibility for accuracy in my work. Once again, our office was set up in a former school building and a girl called Grete joined our team as a replacement for Ditta who had decided not to come with us to the Special Investigations job. Life settled to a steady pace with demanding work to be done, but slowly normality was being re-established in our day-to-day routines. Gradually the stresses of war were retreating as we focused on putting right some of the many injustices that had occurred. Now there was no danger in each day we could feel comfortable and at ease as we enjoyed our freedom once more. Unlike poor Vienna, Graz had been spared the worst of the bombing so there was not so much structural rebuilding to do here. However, the people themselves had to start rebuilding their lives and that was a difficult task for those who had been traumatized and shattered by the war.

Given the relative safety of Graz, Captain Galliford felt it possible for his wife and two boys to join him. The family were accommodated in a large and beautiful suite in the best hotel in Graz which was very comfortable and luxurious. Not only was I employed in my usual work, but I would frequently be asked to look after the little boys, Brian and Roger. I remember spending many happy days with the family and we established a firm friendship which lasted for years.

I continued to work with the SIB in Graz until I married Jim, a Quartermaster Sergeant with the British Military Police, in August 1949. I was 20 years old. The future looked good and I anticipated a time when we would live in England and my dreams would finally come true. The past was behind me, as it was for everyone who had experienced the horrors of war. I had no wish to look back. I was embarking on a new and exciting chapter in my life and I was determined to make the most of whatever adventures lay ahead.

Chapter 11

The Girl with The Golden Smile

The end of the Second World War in Europe and its inevitable outcome for Nazi Germany came as a huge relief to the young Milly Keller. For Milly there was little to resist other than the attentions of the hordes of very good-looking young Allied service personnel who were now entering Innsbruck as part of a new Allied occupation force. Like a great many Austrians Milly and her family yearned for things to get back to normal, yet it was clear it would be some time before the normality they knew before the war could return to Austria. Innsbruck had suffered from the effects of heavy Allied bombing, yet as soon as the last shots died down the citizens of Innsbruck began to rebuild shattered homes along with shattered lives. For Milly herself the years following 1945 were ones of adolescent discovery and adventure. Milly was 13, now a teenager: for the greater part of her young life she had only ever known war. To those Milly referred to as her family and friends she was often known as 'the girl with the golden smile'. Milly had grown into a very pretty young girl and was often the subject of much envy from her close friends as a result. Milly's childhood friend, Rolf Schildt, recalled:

She had always been a very pretty girl. She had lovely eyes and hair and she always wore these nice little dress outfits even when she came out to play when we were kids. Her father was friends with my father, and both worked at the railway yard in the city. We local boys would always fight over who was going to knock on the door of her house to ask her out to play in the street. We used to play much the same kinds of games that kids played in England

– football, tag and also a game called kiss chase. With friends like Milly Keller around the kiss chase game was always going to be very popular for obvious reasons [laughs]. Though she only ever kissed us boys on the cheek and that was only when there was no danger of anyone seeing. When Hitler's army entered Austria and the war began to affect our lives, we couldn't go to school some days and we couldn't even go outside as we used to and play in the streets as it became too dangerous. When we did meet up, we both shared the same concerns for our dear fathers as the railways at Innsbruck were a constant target for the Allied planes. So, as the war progressed, we saw less of each other. I remember in 1944 the bombing increased and it was particularly bad. We had to leave our city homes for these camps in the countryside areas outside the danger zone. There were a number of these camps as one camp would never have catered for everyone, so several were set up outside the city. The farming people of Innsbruck were the unsung heroes of the community. They converted their barns and storage sheds into accommodation for us. I remember each morning the older men leaving these farms heading off to work to the railway – all the other young men had been called up to fight. Many of us by this time were sick of the death and destruction that Adolf Hitler and his Nazi Party had brought upon us in Austria. I know my parents didn't support what Hitler was doing and Milly told me her mother wasn't happy with it all either. Milly's father was – how do we say? – 'on the fence' regarding the Hitler regime: he just wanted to keep working and so towed the line. I guess you couldn't blame him for that. I remember after the war had ended Milly told me that she had once put sugar in the fuel tank of one of the German trucks when they came through Innsbruck. I said to her, 'That wouldn't have worked,' to which she replied, 'Oh yes it did! It clogged their fuel lines and my father saw it broken down at the roadside a short distance outside Innsbruck.' I said to her, 'That was a very dangerous thing to have done. Do you know what they would have done to you if they had caught you?' She didn't seem troubled by that thought at all and said, 'Yes, I know what they would have done to me.' On reflection it was one tiny droplet, a tiny little act of what was resistance, or sabotage even. I greatly admired this pretty girl for her brave and impulsive action as it showed certain courageous qualities in her personality that I respected.

Following the end of the war some difficult years lay ahead, not just for Milly Keller but for many of Austria's liberated citizens. Milly recalls:

There were some very tough years to get through with much work to be done. I was still young yet had no real ideas of what I wanted to do for work and things. Now the Nazis were gone I could do anything I wanted to do within reason – I was free to decide my own destiny. I was very lucky: had the Nazis won the war I would have had no choice other than to be forced into being Nazi 'breeding stock'. Yes, I knew what their plans were for us so-called 'special girls': it became obvious after a while what it was all about. I thank God that it never happened, and Hitler had been stopped. I used to speak with some of the German-speaking Allied soldiers, and they would ask me what I wanted to do in life for a job. I told them I had no idea. When I was 17, I began working at a post office in Innsbruck which I enjoyed as it was a very social job working closely with the community. Things took time to return to what we would call normal after the war. Houses and infrastructures destroyed in the bombing all had to be rebuilt and we all had to play a part in that, even if it was just clearing rubble, we did our bit. As our community got back on its feet in the summer, we would have our folk festivals. These festivals went on throughout the summertime and were celebrated in various forms in cities, towns and villages all over Austria. They were not just an excuse to get drunk and many had local traditional significance such as celebrating the end of the harvest and things like that. I remember while working at the post office at Innsbruck meeting a girl named Martha who was a year younger than me. She came to the post office regularly through the week and we got talking on the subject of the local folk festivals. The inns that provided the alcohol in the form of the local and regional beers always needed girls to serve the customers at these events. Martha asked me if I would be interested in working with her at a big upcoming event at Munich. At first, I was very hesitant, yet my sense for a bit of adventure got the better of me and so I decided to go with her once everything had been agreed. My parents – Father in particular – was not happy about me going to some festival where drunken men might leer at me. Yet I had made up my mind and the weekend's work would give me some much-needed extra income to supplement my post office wages. Martha told me that I would not need many clothes as traditional dress was to be provided and this was what we would have to wear. The dresses we would be wearing were known as a *Dirndl*. This was a traditional style of dress worn by females in Bavaria and Austria and modelled on the kind of traditional dress that female peasants wore in those regions. I had seen them many times but had never worn one in my life up until this point, so I felt quite excited about it. So, with my little adventure beginning, Martha and I caught the train to Munich where we would be spending the weekend. When we arrived at Munich Martha had someone waiting to pick us up by car and take us to this ancient, rickety, old-looking inn. It was a typical old public house, as you would call them in England. It was not far outside Munich, yet the countryside made you feel you were in the middle of nowhere. When we arrived, there was already a celebration going on and we could see people dancing and having a good time. Many of the locals were wearing traditional costumes for the event and it felt like we were stepping back in time. We took our cases containing the few things we needed for the weekend and the owner of this small establishment, an ageing man I guessed to have been in his late fifties who introduced himself as Herr Gunther Weiss, showed us to a tiny room in the attic with two single beds arranged side by side. It was comfortable enough for us as we had slept in worse places than this during the war. We were asked if we had eaten anything and we told him no, so he immediately arranged some food for us which we thought very kind of the man. It was his wife – a lady named Engela or Angela, I can't remember which it was now, but anyway it was she – who brought us some food to one of the tables downstairs. We sat eating and looking around us. The inn had a cosy feel to it – there was a big open fire at its centre and a taxidermy bear stood in one corner. There were shields and swords adorning the walls and it felt like we were in some medieval building; it was quite wonderful. When we finished eating, we were both given the *Dirndl* dresses to put on. Martha struggled to get into hers as it was a tiny bit small for her but, with my help, we managed to get her into the dress, laughing hysterically in the process. Then it was my turn. I had visions of the dress not fitting correctly and making me look as if I was walking around in an army tent or something. As it happened the dress fitted me very well and, once we were ready, we went downstairs ready to start working. As we walked through the inn, Herr Weiss called us both over. We wondered what he wanted and then he looked down at our footwear and said, 'Hmm, you can't wear those – they look ridiculous!' pointing at my brown leather sandals and Martha's black walking boots. Then Herr Weiss insisted, 'It's very warm out there. Can't you take those off, and the socks too?' So, we perched on the bench beside the bar and took off our shoes and socks then we stood up and asked, 'Okay, is this better?' He stood looking at us admiringly before saying, 'Yes, that's it! You could actually pass for two Bavarian peasant girls now!' He smiled then sent us out into the large garden at the back where all the guests were drinking and dancing. Did we look what they call 'sexy' today? I guess with hindsight that we must have done with our busts straining to remain within the confines of our bodices and with bare legs. Most of the men there were present with their wives and there were very strict rules back then that anyone touching us or making inappropriate advances would be banned, so we were quite safe from any lecherous or amorous advances from the local male populace! We served the local beer, which in England is known as lager, and there were white and red wines available too for the ladies. We served the beers in the traditional beer stein, a large heavy glass that held two pints of the beer. We had been shown how to carry these large, heavy vessels and it took some considerable effort at first to do so without spilling anything. Once you got the knack of it you could carry two full steins of beer in each hand. Even the local women drank from these glasses and by evening everyone was quite intoxicated and, as traditional instruments were played in the garden, everyone danced and celebrated. At the end of the evening Martha and I were both shattered and just wanted our beds, but Herr Weiss wasn't having any of it and insisted we join him, his wife and the guests for some beer. He asked me, 'Have you ever drunk beer before, my young lady?' Not wishing to appear naïve, I replied, 'Yes, of course I have, sir.' I wished I had kept my mouth shut as the next thing I knew Martha and I were sitting at the table outside each with a huge stein of beer before us. I remember thinking to myself, 'Oh, my God – if only my parents could see me now!' I took some rather pathetic little sips from the endless lake of beer in my glass while Martha took large gulps of the amber-coloured liquid. As she drank, she looked at me and laughed and said, 'You haven't drunk beer before, have you?' I had to admit to her that I hadn't to which she then quipped, 'Oh, you poor thing – you're going to be pissed as a rat if you drink that!' As she gulped down the beer with all the enthusiasm of a man, I watched in awe. She soon emptied her glass then swapped our glasses around so that she had my virtually full glass of beer to drink. I was asked if I wanted another beer to which I replied, 'No, thank you, that was enough for me.' We sat and watched the people dance before we were both asked to join in which we did, and it was very good fun. After the dancing we sat back down, and Martha emptied her second stein of beer, the one that I should have drunk but couldn't. She emptied the last dregs of the beer onto the grass, sat there and let out the loudest belch I had ever heard. Several people looked over towards our table and we burst out laughing. At that we were both more than ready for bed and retired to our room for the evening. The music continued for some time, yet it did not stop us from sleeping. We were soon fast asleep and in no time were being roused on the Sunday morning for a big breakfast which consisted of bread, fried eggs, salami and cheeses washed down with black coffee. There was also orange juice and milk if we wanted it. At midday the little festival continued, and we were again serving beers to the guests. There were many children here this time and they ran around like rabbits, reminding me of my carefree days at Innsbruck before the war. For a moment I began to think about Innsbruck and felt a little homesick, even though Innsbruck was barely an hour away. I was happy when the day was over and I could change back into my normal dress, sandals and socks. My feet were killing me as we had a busy time of it on that Sunday. Before we left for our lift back to Innsbruck, Herr Weiss called us into his parlour out the back and gave us our pay. He told us how much we had earned and to check it carefully before we left and put it somewhere safe. Martha and I were thrilled with the money we had earned and promised Herr Weiss we would come and work for him again if he wanted us. At that we shook hands with him and his wife and got into the car which would take us all the way back to Innsbruck to save us the train fare. When we arrived home, we were greeted like heroes by our families. After this Martha and I became very close friends: we often went clothes shopping in the city or went out to watch movies together. We understood that we had good lives, that there were those in other parts who were not having such a good time. Vienna was occupied by the Russians. It was no secret what they did to our people during the fighting and in the so-called peace after 1945. The crime rate in Vienna after 1945 was horrendous compared to the other occupation zones of Austria. A friend once wrote to me telling me that 90 per cent of acts of criminality in Vienna city were due to Russians. They drank heavily which gave them an appetite for violence and rape. I felt for my poor friend as she had tried to leave the city on three occasions but was denied by the Russian authorities. They didn't take too kindly to people wanting to leave them to go into the western zones. It was all a measure of things to come later really, wasn't it?

It was actually in 1951 – I was 19 years old, and had been out to the movies with Martha one Saturday evening – when I bumped into an old childhood friend who I hadn't seen for a long time. It was a chance meeting and I heard a male voice shouting, 'Milly, Milly Keller!' as we streamed out of the movie house. I stopped and looked to where I could hear this man shouting and saw that it was my old friend Rolf Schildt. I shouted I would see him outside as it was just too crowded at that moment. So, I stood outside with Martha and waited for Rolf to come out. He came running up and threw his arms around me. I was very pleased to see him too as it had been a long time. Martha said to me, 'I'm going home, Milly, but will see you in the week, okay?' I told her she didn't have to go but she insisted that she was tired and was going to bed. So, Rolf and I stood alone together outside the movie house until he asked me if I would like to go for a drink with him. I agreed and off we went. We went into the first bar we came across; I went and took a seat while Rolf bought us drinks.

As we talked, I told him all about the little adventure in Munich and what I had been doing over the years and my job at the post office, just small talk really. As I talked Rolf never took his eyes off me! It was clear that he liked me more than in the 'just good friends' context! At the end of the night he asked me if he could take me out again and I agreed as I liked him very much. We went on a picnic and we both agreed how lucky we were as we could not be enjoying this much freedom had we been under the Communists. We believed back then that it was just a matter of time before another war would break out between the western Allies and Communist Russia. It really did feel an inevitability back then during the early Cold War years. Rolf argued that there were far too many British and American forces in Austria now, that if the Russians made a serious play for territory there they would be met with considerable force and beaten back. Besides, the Americans had the A-Bomb as we called it and the Communists did not. As we picnicked by the lake amongst scenery familiar to us through our childhood, we shared our first romantic kiss.

With hindsight I shouldn't have allowed our romance to blossom in quite the way it did as I knew I was not ready for marriage and children at that time. Although we began making plans to get married the following year, it was in that year, 1952, that I broke off the engagement to Rolf effectively ending our marriage plans. I sensed he was becoming very frustrated with me anyway for various reasons. It was better to end things there than on the day of a wedding at the altar, I thought. While it was briefly painful, and I felt that I had lost a childhood friend forever, it was all soon forgotten. The little bit of travelling I had done with Martha appealed to me. I liked the idea of not being tied to one place and wanted to see more of the world while I was still young enough to do it. Martha knew the English language very well and she endeavoured to teach me English. She told me that if we were to go travelling further than Austria, then we should both be able to understand English as this would be important in getting jobs to provide us with money.

So, from 1952 to 1954 Martha and I travelled much of Europe. Countries in eastern Europe were ones we had no desire to visit at all for obvious reasons and we knew we would not have been safe there. So, we travelled most of western Europe working in bars and restaurants or doing the odd bit of work on the land. Most of western Europe was still in a bad way having been torn apart by the Nazis. Yet, we travelled through France and on into Spain where we spent several months. Spain was beautiful and we both loved its warm, inviting climate which was a huge difference from that of central Europe at that time in winter. It was very easy to find work in Spain and we found the Spanish people very nice. Once we had saved enough money, we headed off again. We had made so many new friends in Spain that we were told if we ever needed to come back there would be jobs waiting for us. When we left Spain, we caught a boat across the Mediterranean to Tunisia, which came as a bit of a shock as there was not much there and the country was very primitive, but it was – what can I say? – a cultural enlightenment for us. We soon realized that we would not be stopping long in countries like Tunisia and ended up going back across the Mediterranean to Italy. After getting off the boat we hitchhiked all the way to Naples. We found most of the Italians more than willing to help us as our Italian was nowhere near as good as our English, but quite a few could speak English. It was now I could see Martha's reasoning in learning English. Again, finding work was not too difficult. The bars, cafés and restaurants were always anxious to pull in two pretty 'German' girls and get them to work for them. Usually, you could get accommodation on the premises where you worked too. On days off we had some of the most beautiful beaches all to ourselves. We would take a picnic basket, bottles of wine and some blankets and spend the whole day swimming and sunbathing. We kept our parents informed of where we were and what we were doing at all times. We understood there were dangers lurking for us in strange countries. We were more than capable of looking after ourselves, but we always let our parents know when we were leaving somewhere and our intended destination. Besides, both mine and Martha's parents enjoyed collecting all the fancy postcards we sent back home.

We returned home to our families for Christmas of 1954 and stayed well into the spring of 1955 picking up casual jobs once again. It was Martha who suggested visiting England. I asked her, 'Are you serious? They will hate us there as we speak like Germans even though we are Austrians.' Martha reassured me that we would be alright and so, nervously, I agreed to go with her. We stayed in Innsbruck for a few more months in order to save up enough money. We also spoke to the many British servicemen we encountered and asked their opinions on things like places to go and places we might find work. Our time in England would be determined by what work we could find, if we could get any that is. Every time we set off, carrying all we needed in backpacks, it felt like we were going on some great adventure. To me – at that time – I couldn't live any other way. The thought of being tied to a home, husband and children filled us both with horror. We knew we couldn't do this forever but for the time being we would travel as much as we could. England was interesting; we went through France and sailed across the English Channel from Calais to Kent on the English coast. As we neared the famed south coast of England I thought back to the war and thought to myself, *Here in the skies above – right here – was where Hitler's Luftwaffe met their fate, where they were defeated!* It was a strange, emotional sensation for us both too.

When we first set foot on English soil it was marvellous. We stayed the night in Kent, one of the most beautiful of English counties. It was full of lush green fields dotted with woods and small coppices with their little farmsteads, villages and church spires poking up from the trees and surrounding hills. As we headed into London the whole dynamic changed: here was a busy fast-moving metropolis bustling with people. We went into several coffee shops enquiring about work but were told there was nothing. We were beginning to feel slightly paranoid about our German-sounding accents when we went into a restaurant bar and asked if there was any work going. The young man behind the counter called the owner of the business who came down from some stairs at the back of the premises. He came up to us saying, 'Ah, good afternoon ladies. What can I do for you both?' We told him we were looking for jobs in London and asked if he had any or knew of any going. We could see that he noticed straight away we had Germanic accents and he asked us where we had come from. We told him, 'We come from Innsbruck, a city in Austria. We aren't Germans.' I think that must have amused him as he smiled. We showed him the identity cards we always carried with us and he could see that we were telling the truth. Either way it landed us a job with a room in which to sleep. London was crazy, very busy particularly in the evenings. In the evening a local English lady came in to work with us. She had that typical cockney accent which was as difficult to understand as ours was to her. She was very kind and helpful though and showed us where all the good shops and the cinemas were in the city. She even showed us around the important landmarks of London, including some places which we had seen in the old Nazi propaganda films of London. Goebbels described it in one of his speeches as 'a city of excess and low morality where wealthy Jews partied and where even the married elite of the country sought the pleasure of whores'. Of course, such remarks were typical of Goebbels' hate speeches. He hated because he was jealous and he would have loved to have lived in the cultural richness that was London himself, only he never got that far, thank God.

We didn't always get things our own way, however, and there were some people who were very rude to us. We would try and explain that we were Austrians, not Germans, and that our country was as much under an occupation against its will as was much of Europe. I remember one old woman saying to us, 'Yes, but you didn't fight back, did you? You all rolled over and welcomed the Germans in.' It was then I told her that there was a resistance movement which did gather some strength in the final part of war and I told her about when I shoved sugar in the petrol tank of a German truck towing an artillery gun; how many of us hated Hitler and the Nazis. Then her anger abated to a degree and we sat down and she told us tales of the London Blitz, the V-1 and V-2 attacks. We both sat listening intently, eager to learn of the suffering of these proud Londoners. It was quite one of the oddest conversations we ever had in England. It was this old lady who then asked us if we had ever experienced 'pie and mash' as she called it. We told her we hadn't heard of it and she told us we must go to Cooke's which was the oldest pie and mash shop in the city. So, two days later we went to this shop which was like a pub, only it didn't serve beer – it served this pie and mash with what they called a 'liquor' which was made from the juices of river eels. As we sat awaiting this local delicacy, we were unsure whether we were going to like it. Martha reminded me, 'Well, after some of that food we had to endure in Tunisia, surely this can't be anywhere near as revolting.' When the pie and mash was placed before us the lady told us, 'There you go, enjoy girls!' So, we got 'stuck in', as they say in London. It was actually very nice and not what we had expected at all, even the liquor made from eels. By the time we had finished we felt fat and our plates were clean. We thanked the lady who had served us and as we did so we were again asked, 'Are you from Germany?' to which we replied, as we walked out of the door, 'No, we aren't Germans, we are from Innsbruck in Austria.' Our time in London was overall very enjoyable, yet there was still so much we wanted to see of this country. We discussed going to Scotland as we so wanted to go there but travelling there would have meant many hours on the road and on trains and it was just not possible at that time. We promised ourselves we could come back one day to see the sights there. Sadly, we never did get to experience Scotland. We found London very expensive even back in those days and despite living above where we worked rent-free, money was always tight.

We both returned home to Innsbruck in the summer of 1957. When I returned home and decided that, at the age of 25, I was going to get a job and settle down for a while to spend time with my family, I had no idea that fate would again alter the course of my life. I managed to get a job at the bank in Innsbruck. They needed someone who could speak fluent English who could act as a liaison between Austrian and British concerns in the city. It was quite an important role and I felt I was more than up for the challenge and the pay was very good. I settled down into my work which I enjoyed and, with my good pay, had started to make plans to rent my own home. I met up with Martha frequently and we went out to bars and restaurants and enjoyed a wonderful social life. During the winter of that year I had just secured my own rented accommodation and had settled in. It was a Saturday night and the city was bustling with activity and excitement: Martha wanted to go out and asked me to join her. I was reluctant at first as I had just had a bath and was about to paint my toenails while listening to some music on my wireless set. Martha was persistent though and, in the end, I decided to get dressed and go out with her if only to shut her up and stop her nagging that I was becoming a hermit! We decided to go and see a movie called *Beneath the Palms on the Blue Sea*. It was a rather 'cheesy' musical and I felt myself falling asleep. In fact, Martha had to nudge me several times as I drifted off. As the credits for the film began to roll, I was somewhat relieved and was glad to get out of what was an unpleasantly smoke-filled 'flea bitten joint'. As we walked down the road, we decided to have dinner and drinks at a restaurant, so we went in and sat down and perused the menu. I was shocked when the young man who came to take our food orders was none other than young Rolf Schildt. I was as surprised to see him as he was me and we both babbled our words at first, but I stood and gave him a hug and asked him how he was getting on and if he had married yet. He smiled at me and said, 'No, I've not married yet and I was rather hoping that there was still a chance for us.' His words took me by surprise, and I didn't know what to say. He appeared different this time around. He took our order and off he went, yet I watched him each time he came out taking food to the customers and taking empty plates and glasses away. I tried to make it obvious that I wasn't watching him, but Martha said, 'You still like that boy, don't you?' I admitted that, yes, I felt differently about him now from the way I did back then. Before we left Rolf came over to our table and he asked me if I would be interested in going to watch a movie with him again and then have dinner afterwards. I told him, 'Yes, I'd love to, provided that the film is not that hogwash that we've just had to sit through!' He smiled broadly and promised he would never inflict that dreadful movie on me. We arranged a date and we went and watched a movie, and then had a lovely dinner afterwards followed by some drinks. Rolf walked me back to my flat but, like a true gentleman, he left me at the door and did not assume he would be spending the night with me, which I thought was very sweet of him. I kissed him on the mouth, and it was then he became quite emotional and told me that he still loved me and asked if there was any chance that I still had feelings for him. I told him that yes, things were different now and that I did have feelings for him; I was older and more mature and had done a lot of the things I had dreamed about doing and that I was now ready to settle down. He then asked me, 'Does that mean there is a chance you will be mine again?' to which I replied, 'If you can forgive me for casting you off in the past then yes there is.' We both agreed we would take things slowly and if we still felt the same in a year or so we would look at getting married. Bless his heart, he jumped for joy and we embraced again and shared a proper kiss on my doorstep.

Two years on, rather later than we had planned, we were married at Innsbruck and moved into one of the new two-bedroomed houses there. Eight months later I discovered I was expecting our first child; we were both so thrilled and our families too. Our first child was a boy, whom we named Karl, and the following year I fell pregnant again. I was so hoping that this time we would be blessed with a daughter and my dreams were answered when I gave birth to a baby girl whom I decided to name Alessa. I was quite happy with having just the two children and didn't really want any more. Rolf would have liked to have had more but in the end, I got my own way. While the children were little, I had to give up my work at the bank. Once they were both at 'first school', it was easier for me to return to work for a few hours a day. Back then it was the fashion that many wives had to have their husband's permission to go to work. Rolf was never like that: if I wanted to go to work, he never once questioned it. Rolf did very well at the restaurant he worked at and was promoted to assistant manager, though this meant at busy times we did not see much of him.

Over the years together we have learned that life is all about 'give and take'. You work together through the rough times and the good times and, overall, we had a very good married life together. I feel that I did all I needed to do after the experiences of the Second World War, I felt ready to settle down when I did, and I have no regrets in my life as a result. I saw a good part of the world through my travelling. There are young people today who haven't seen as much of the world as I have. We have a beautiful world here where we can all live together, yet there will always be those who don't want that. There will always be wars due to greed, religion and money, sadly.

Rolf Schildt concurs with his now-elderly wife Milly and adds:

Milly has not always been the easiest of women to live with: she has always been very strong-willed and maybe I have always been a bit stubborn; the two are not always a good combination in a marriage [laughs]. But despite our occasional differences I could love no woman any more in life than the woman I have always called 'the girl with the golden smile' – my childhood friend, Milly Keller.

Chapter 12

An Inglorious End

For Ellie Bergmann and her mother, the end of the war brought about an anxious wait for news of a father and husband. Ellie recalls:

The wounded soldiers began to arrive back in Vienna via trains. I remember each morning my mother would take me with her to the station in the city where we would wait anxiously, watching the soldiers disembark on the platform. The soldiers appeared thoroughly beaten and dejected. Most were of Austrian birth who had been drafted after the Anschluss. Each day we would go to the station only to return in silence feeling that ours was going to be a hopeless situation with a sad outcome. It must have been on the third week of this dreadful waiting on the platform that my mother spotted Father getting off one of the trains. My mother screamed with emotion as she saw him. He looked alright, but his arm was in a sling. When he saw us both he broke down with emotion: it was the first time I had ever seen my father cry – in fact, I had never seen any man cry like he did that morning. We stood there for a few minutes in this silent embrace apart from my father's tears then we walked home. Over the days and weeks that followed it was a battle to regain a degree of family normality. My father had a broken arm which required frequent medical attention to check its progress. I remember him at the kitchen table telling Mother about his capture by the Red Army, how in his own words he was treated fairly well although was beaten up at first. When questioned by the Russians, my father explained that he had been drafted and that he had not wanted to fight for the Nazis. He was questioned quite intensely as were all Wehrmacht prisoners. I think he understood how lucky he had been as most of the Wehrmacht soldiers taken by the Russians were transported back to Siberia for forced labour. Many were not released until years after the war and thousands died in captivity. Why they let my father go, amongst others, I cannot be sure. Maybe it was because they could see in his eyes that he was telling them the truth – I don't know. Other than that, I would sit and help nurse him back to health while my mother took on jobs to help support us. All the time I was with Father I would try and ask him about his war and the fighting, but it was very difficult for him to talk about it without breaking down. I didn't want to upset him or cause him any further pain, so I stopped asking him questions. All I remember him saying about it was, 'It was savage. We lived, fought and died as if animals. It was inhumane and beyond the endurance of even the fittest and bravest of men.' He told me they, the Russians, drove their tanks over enemy soldiers and that he had stared death in the face on so many occasions that he no longer feared death or dying.

As a young girl all of this was hard to take in and it was only over time that I began to understand what men like my father had been through. It was not long after we got Father back that problems began at night. My bedroom was right next to that of my parents. I remember it so vividly as if it were yesterday when it started. I was awoken with a terrible fright to the sound of shouting and crying. It was in the middle of the night and being startled awake like that was horrible. My heart was racing as I jumped out of my bed and called for my mother as I was frightened. All I remember is Mother saying, 'It's okay, Ellie, your father has had a bad dream. Now please go back to sleep.' I would lie there until my heart stopped pounding and then would struggle to get back to sleep again. This same thing would happen regularly over the nights that followed, and, in the end, I was sent to stay with my aunt and uncle. I didn't want to go as I felt I could support Mother more by being there with her, but she insisted.

The time I spent with my aunt, uncle and two cousins was really very nice and I stayed with them for a month before I returned home. I was scared at what might have happened while I had been away. Mother looked drained and I did all I could to help as much as possible. It was then that my mother was taken ill: she collapsed one morning and couldn't stop crying. I was scared and called for our neighbour, a kindly lady named Frau Lindner, who took my mother to her house while I looked after Father. My mother had suffered a mental breakdown and she had to go away to convalesce for a few weeks and receive treatment. I told her I would look after Father and he would be alright in my care. As my father's health and broken arm steadily improved, he was able to do more, yet all of the cooking, cleaning and washing was done by me. I recall after our meal one evening my father said, 'My little angel, I am so proud of you. You shouldn't have to be doing this – you are just a child. I'm sorry.' I told him not to be so silly and that I was fine. Those were very hard days indeed, but we were not the only family to be dealing with things like this.

When Mother came back home, she looked much better, but I was determined that I would do all I could to help her and continued to do much of the work around the house. My grandparents did all they could too and as a family we all rallied round. My grandfather would still call round to our house when he was able and take me out with him in the car. It was about this time that he began to give me serious driving lessons. I picked it up very quickly and I really enjoyed it, but I never actually drove off anywhere solo until I was 17 years of age, by which time I was, of course, very experienced and competent! My father continued to suffer with his night terrors, but they were steadily becoming less intense and he was able to deal with it without waking up the whole house and the street!

Frau Lindner was a wonderful woman and she helped me so much and I learned a lot from her. She gave me some tuition in French, English and Spanish. She had been a teacher in her younger days, and I would often sit in her living room with her while she told me stories about her life before the Germans invaded. It was Frau Lindner who taught me the importance of educating oneself and learning as much as possible, and how this would help sometime in life. It was thanks to this wonderful, warm and caring woman that I later worked briefly as a translator for the Allied forces in Austria. I was 16 at the time and worked firstly for the staff under General Marie Bethouart in the French sector. I enjoyed this work immensely even though it meant being away from home for a long period of time. My parents were anxious that I should leave Vienna and, despite relations between the Russian occupying forces and the locals improving steadily over the months and years after 1945, my parents were still very nervous of the future.

It was through this work as a kind of liaison person translating documents and live conversations between the French and Austrian forces that I met my first and only sweetheart. It was not the most romantic of first introductions as I thought him very arrogant and aloof at first sight. He was a French corporal named Vincent Faucheux. I knew he liked me as he had made this very obvious, and I liked him too. There was a five-year age gap between us but in the end this didn't really matter and he asked me if I would go out with him for dinner one evening, and I accepted after making it perfectly clear I was no 'easy girl' looking for casual romance! He assured me he was perfectly serious and of good intentions and I took his word on it. As it happened our little date was wonderful, and he behaved like the perfect gentleman. He was so different from how I saw him in our working capacity

where I had always thought him a bit arrogant. We talked about
the war, our experiences and what life had been like in the Soviet
sector of my country. I told him I didn't want the Russians being
there, that – like the Germans – they were now the new occupying
force and one which had beaten our men, raped our females and
generally terrorized our neighbourhoods. I told him that they
were not people one would normally associate with liberation.
In fact, he began asking so many questions I actually asked him,
'Are you a spy or something? Are you spying on me?' Of course
he thought that was hilarious and assured me he was no secret
agent trying to get information from me. I may have been young,
but I had a very good way of sensing people; I could generally
tell a bad person from a good one – it's all in their manner and
their eyes in particular. After all, I had been around enough evil
to be able to recognize it when I saw it. As he sat across the table
from me in the restaurant, I stared into his eyes intently. I think
this made him a little nervous but, as I said, his manners were
wonderful and he was very kind. After our dinner date he walked
me back to the small chalet where I was staying with some other
young women. As we stood in the doorway a couple of French
women walked by; they must have heard my accent as one made
a derogatory remark about Vincent supposedly 'sleeping with an
old enemy'! It didn't really worry me, but it showed feelings were
still raw and one still had to be careful. Vincent kissed my hand
and bid me a goodnight and I admired the fact he didn't act in a
'pushy' manner, and I respected him even more for that.

I travelled back home frequently to visit my parents as I always
worried about them and how they were coping. Thankfully,
I found them to be in good spirits under the circumstances.
I told them about my French corporal friend, as I referred to
him. Immediately, Father raised his eyebrows warning me about
these French 'Romeos' as he called them. I assured him I was
not doing anything stupid and that his intentions were perfectly

honourable. I was more concerned for my parents than anything. The situation in Vienna was not good after 1945. Although the discipline among the Russian troops there improved, there were still economic worries and unemployment issues which would need to be addressed. After the war my mother took on two jobs until my father was fully fit again and he returned to his blacksmithing work which he enjoyed greatly. My pay from working as a translator wasn't great but I was able to buy things which I could then take home. Vincent also helped and the first time he came home with me to meet my parents, which was shortly after my seventeenth birthday, he brought a box of goods which he then gave to them. I think my father was shocked by Vincent's generosity and his genuine concern and this really helped break the ice between Vincent and my parents. By the time we had to leave Vienna, my parents could see that this young man was probably the best thing that had happened to their daughter. He promised them he would look after me with his life. I don't know, I just totally fell in love with him, yet it was a steady courtship which matured over the few years after we had met. We got to know one another first which couples these days don't seem interested in doing. Vincent often talked about marriage and children and I think he was trying to find out how I felt about these things. I told him I would like children of my own and to settle down and live a happy life – that is all I had ever wanted, I didn't want anything else.

For most of my youth I had only ever known war. I had experienced war in its full fury, as had many other young people in Austria and it was something that left its mark on us all. However hard we tried to forget the horrors that occurred under the Nazis and those that followed with the Russian occupation, there are still times when I sit down and think back to those times and I shed a few tears. I shed tears for all those people who were taken from our communities by the Germans. Many of these people were ones I grew up with and went to school with. Their only crime was that they did not fit the racial criteria of that monster, Hitler. I don't even know what happened to many of them. I assume most were sent to the camps – hellholes such as Mauthausen or the Lodz Ghetto before being sent on to Auschwitz. All I do know is that very few came back from these places, and those that did suffered physically and mentally from their ill treatment and experiences for the remainder of their lives. We all hoped that when the Russian forces came into Austria, they would behave differently towards us, but sadly they didn't. In their eyes we were all Nazis, which of course we were not. There were many who helped in the Austrian resistance in many different ways. The resistance were the unsung heroes of Austria. It didn't matter what they did or how little they did to resist the Nazis by fighting back in a covert manner. Their actions showed the world that not all of us were sympathetic to what the Germans were doing in Europe.

I can say that overall I have had a good life. Vincent and I married and had three lovely children. Vincent remained in the military for many years after our marriage as it was the job he loved. I stayed at home and raised our children and was happy being an 'army wife'. We moved back to Vienna in 1958 so I could be closer to my parents and grandparents. By this time the city had changed, the Russians were gone and we felt that it was now our country again. I understood that the stigma of what Germany was responsible for would last a lifetime. How could those crimes of such huge proportions ever be forgotten, and it is only right that we should all remember what happened during the terrible years. People should also remember there were many good people in Austrian society, some of them very young who did much good despite all the horrors going on around them. Again, I say those who actively resisted against Nazism in our country, however young or however old they may have been, were incredibly brave, honourable people and were the real heroes. Sadly, few will ever receive any recognition for their deeds back in those dark days of war, and many do not, to this day, wish to seek any reward as such. Sadly, today, we exist in a culture where if a celebrity takes his or her clothes off on TV, they get an award or their own talk show. It is worth remembering that the real heroes of our past and indeed present are in some instances ordinary humble people whose names you will have never heard quoted in the press or on TV. I am thankful, I have had a good life overall.

When people today ask me about Hitler and the Nazis and what it was like having to live under their rule, I tell them, 'It was a dreadful experience, and when the end came and it was all over, it felt as if one was witnessing the funeral of someone who you hated.' There was nothing glorious about Hitler, the Nazis or their Third Reich. Anyone who does think it was glorious is very lucky to have not lived under it, that's all I can say to them. When it ended it was far from pleasant, it was in every sense an inglorious ending. I sometimes think back to those days, but it makes me cry. I would rather sit and look at my garden, the wildlife around me and my family, than think back to those days. I hope by telling you all that I have told you I can now close that chapter, leave it all behind and not have to talk of it any more.

Epilogue: My Wonderful Life

For all the women whose stories have been recounted, the war years had a profound effect on their lives, affecting them so emphatically at such an impressive stage in their adolescence and robbing them of many years which should have been filled with the joy of discovering an exciting and wonderful world. How incredible it is that these women should have picked up the pieces of their fragmented lives and striven to overcome their traumas to build a fulfilling future.

Herti's sense of adventure and determination was instrumental in the way she moved forward positively with her life after the war. She kept her promise to her father, even after her move to the UK, maintaining contact with her mother and sister and making sure they were looked after. Herti describes the events of her life in England, always with a sense of disbelief that her life could have proved so wonderful in spite of the terrible war years. She remembers the happiness of her early years and she expresses genuine amazement that she was able to rebuild her life and achieve such joy over the following decades. Here is the rest of her story:

For the first year of our married life Jim and I lived in Vienna. Jim had returned briefly to the UK to be 'de-mobbed' and obtained employment in Austria for a British company selling quality cloth. I had remained working in Graz until Jim came back and we set up home in Vienna. On 1 April 1950 we moved to London and my long-held plan to get to England became a reality! We lived in a maisonette in West Kensington having accommodation on the ground and first floors of a large house. Jim worked as a security officer for three adjacent stores in Kensington High Street. I quickly obtained employment in a number of short-term posts before becoming an office manager with British Home Stores in Fulham and soon after was offered a position as trainee store manager with Dorothy Perkins in Croydon. I was quickly promoted to manageress at the Fulham branch – I remember that the 'takings' in the branch doubled during my first three months there and this impressed the directors enormously! I was sent as a 'trouble-shooter' to various branches that were struggling with the task of 'turning them around'. I stayed with Dorothy Perkins until 1966 when I was offered a post with British Airways (then BOAC). By this time, I knew I needed a change in my life and, in spite of being offered considerable promotion to stay with 'DP', I decided to take on this new challenge.

Although my working life had given me plenty of opportunities, I had felt for some time that my personal life was not really going anywhere. Jim and I did not have a family and I continued to do all I could to support my mother and sister at home in Austria. Jim was almost twice my age when we married – I was 20 and he was 35 – and as the years had gone by I came to realize that whilst he was content to live quietly and unadventurously, I could see the years slipping away and there was so much I felt I wanted to do and see in the world. So, I made the decision to leave Jim and after several years – he did not want this separation – I obtained a divorce. We did remain on friendly terms, however, until his death in 1989.

In February 1974 I married Doug. We had met some years before and had gradually established a wonderful relationship which lasted for forty-six happy and eventful years. When we were first together Doug worked in finance, but his real love was in art and particularly antiquarian books. We lived in Hampstead Garden Suburb, in north London, where Doug had spent all his life, and when an opportunity arose for him to acquire a gallery there he leapt at the chance. From then on, he lived his dream of buying and selling wonderful art, specializing in Victorian watercolours and oil paintings. Doug had a workshop opposite the gallery where he carried out framing and repairs. We had wonderful friends and neighbours and we enjoyed a full and active social life. London was a treasure trove of art and culture which we explored whenever we could. With Doug, I could sing and dance again!

Meanwhile my career with BA continued to expand. I worked mainly at Heathrow airport for many years as part of the Passenger Services team supporting customers. I dealt with tricky situations and met some very interesting people, including politicians, celebrities and royalty from across the globe. One of the benefits of working for BA was that Doug and I had many opportunities to travel, of which we took full advantage. At one point I 'commuted' to Paris to work for six months.

In 1986 I decided to take early retirement but this did not last long. I was approached by a friend and asked if I would take on a part-time job as a tour guide with groups of school children. This was a very enjoyable role and I had a wonderful time with many young students and their teachers from all over the UK, seeing the sights and exploring the capital. However, British Airways called me back and I accepted a job with BA Holidays which was based in a number of London hotels. So much for being retired – I was now back working full-time!

I had worked for BA between 1966 and 1994 when Doug and I decided we would move to Cornwall. Aged 65, I was pleased to qualify for retirement, but BA was reluctant to let me go. I was offered a series of six-monthly contracts to stay working with them and I agreed to extend my working life for the first six months, commuting to London each week from our new home in Mullion. However, when I was finally 'free', I found that, somehow, I had another job – this time in a large retail department store in Truro. I had noticed an advertisement and decided to apply, thinking that I would enjoy a new challenge in the retail fashion world. As I was over 65, I 'reduced' my age by ten years and got the job, which lasted from 1994 to 2000 when at last I finished my working life. Then in 2009, I was approached yet again and asked if I would consider working for a ladies' fashion store in Truro – where it was assumed I was a sprightly 70-year-old. I decided not to resume my career but was flattered and amused by the offer. Doug enjoyed boasting to all his friends that his wife had been 'head-hunted' for a new employment opportunity at 80 years of age!

Throughout my life I have always loved music and dancing. Some of my earliest memories are closely connected to music and precious times spent with my family. My piano was a treasured gift and gave me enormous joy. In later years, Doug and I gained much pleasure from attending concerts at Truro Cathedral. However, since Doug died, I have found it difficult to listen to beautiful music which brings back so many wonderful memories yet reminds me of so many losses and makes me feel sad. Essentially, I am a happy and optimistic person and always have been, so I choose not to dwell on my losses but to focus on the good things in life. If this means I have to sacrifice the pleasure of music, so be it.

The war years affected my growing up greatly: since the age of 5 I had longed for a career in medicine and planned to complete my schooling in Graz and from there to study at Heidelberg University in order to become a doctor. All these ambitions were thwarted by the Nazis and my formal education came to a halt when I was fifteen. Looking back, it was a shame that I was unable to pursue my dream but it was in my nature to make the best of opportunities that came my way and I feel certain that it was my sense of positivity that enabled me to make the most of my life and not to waste valuable time worrying about what was no longer possible. Also, the deprivations and horrors of war gave me a sense of perspective – a realization of what is truly important. Having witnessed the survivors of the concentration camps, how could one ever feel anything but gratitude for the abundance of good things life has given me?

One of life's great pleasures for both Doug and me was to travel far and wide. We had so many fabulous holidays abroad – in America, India, Greece, Italy, France, Belgium, Switzerland, Barbados and Africa, for example. Always we would explore independently, hiring cars and driving off into the unknown. In Kenya we were 'at one' with nature, wondering at the magnificence of the great animals and feeling the insignificance of human life compared with the rich wealth of the animal kingdom. We were in awe of this magical continent. Something similar happened to us in India and in other places where we found ourselves removed from 'civilization' – truly, these remarkable experiences gave us an abundance of happiness.

I have always loved driving, too, and remember fondly the cars I have owned and the fun I have had! How I enjoyed nipping around in my MGBGT! I drove all over Europe, thinking nothing of going to pick up my mother and niece from their home in Graz and bringing them back to England for a holiday. I considered myself to be a good driver, too, so imagine my surprise to be pulled over once by a policeman in London who then told me he had been following me for some time but wanted to tell me that I was an excellent driver! That surely was a 'first'! Even very recently I have driven all over Devon and Cornwall, navigating some precipitous hills and narrow lanes. I will happily jump in the car and visit friends who are miles away and have to be reminded from time to time that perhaps I should slow down a bit – in my activities, not mph!

My other great love in life has always been animals of the domestic kind. My early memory of being with the horses at my grandparents' house is still as clear today as it was then. I can close my eyes and visualize lying down in a field next to one of the horses and snuggling close, smelling that wonderful 'horsey' aroma that gave me such comfort and warmth. And, of course, dogs too have given me great joy: Doug and I had several wonderful pets and we also cared for many other dogs belonging to friends when they went away. Even now I cannot say no if someone asks me to help out for a week or two, though I have to leave the dog walking along the Cornish cliffs to others these days.

So I wake each day and think how lucky I am to enjoy good health, many friends, a comfortable home, a lovely community and plenty of activities to keep me occupied – I look forward to my weekly Scrabble sessions and have recently joined a book group, as well as having completed an IT course. Life is full; life is rich; life is happy. I sit in my garden in summer or in my armchair on winter evenings and close my eyes and think back over my life – a rich tapestry of people, places and events all woven into the fabric that has shaped the person I am. The music continues to play, and I dance on.

Afterword

ll I would like to reiterate in my afterword for this wonderful volume is that it has been a real pleasure to have had a part in its creation. Herti Bryan's story is as unique as the lady herself. I know that having to read through the manuscript for this work brought back all kinds of happy memories for Herti, but also some very painful ones, so much so that they, and the stories of the other women who survived the atrocities of occupation, actually made her feel ill. In a sense retracing the steps through her childhood and youth, firstly under the Nazis and then the Russians, has been a journey of both joy and pain in equal measure. Yet this was a story that had to be presented to the world of military and social history literature. I also have immense admiration for the other contributors who gave their stories for inclusion in this work, once bright young individuals who, like Herti, recognized that the Nazis and their Third Reich was nothing other than an empire of evil in which prejudice and murder became an acceptable means of controlling the people. No matter where darkness falls upon any nation the light of good will always shine through. To Herti, and indeed all of the contributors to this book who chose to make their stand against the oppression and murder which tore their country apart so long ago now, it has been a pleasure to have known and worked alongside you all.

Tim Heath
January 2020

* * *

Exploring eighty-plus years of memory with Herti has been a journey filled with emotion. Certainly, the early memories were ones of joy and happiness but, as we progressed through the years, there were moments of difficulty as she relived the traumatic experiences of her adolescent years. I was amazed at the clarity of Herti's recollections: sometimes there would be moments of doubt before suddenly everything became clear. I would read back to her what I had written and she would exclaim, 'That's it! That's just how it happened!' Small details of each 'chapter' would come into her mind as if she were reliving the past. Occasionally, there would be some confusion about sequences of events or names of people but, on the whole, Herti's ability to recall the events of her life is quite remarkable. Inevitably there are some 'gaps' in her story and often she would say, 'I wonder what happened to him [or her]. Wouldn't it be marvellous to know?' We have written her story as fully and as accurately as possible but, just maybe, someone will read this book and have some answers to her questions. Herti left Austria with very few possessions – her home had been bombed, destroying much of what the family had and, when she ran out of the back door to escape the Russians entering at the front, she had nothing but the summer clothes she stood up in. Relying totally on her memory and a handful of early photographs, we have been able to reconstruct the story of her remarkable life and fulfil her ambition to record this important chapter of history.

Virginia Wells
January 2020

Acknowledgements

I would like to thank the following for their most valued assistance during the writing of this work:

Amelia 'Milly' Keller, Hilde Schubert, Ingrid Hoess, the families of Ingeborg Schauss (née Nietzer) and Anders Bilch, Lance-Sergeant Erich Child, Elizabeth 'Ellie' Bergmann and Karl Voght. Any material which required translation into English language was translated by Anthony Schilabo, Dieter Perez and Marianna Goetze.

Tim Heath

In addition, Herti wishes to thank those who supported her in the writing of her story, namely:

Frank Millard, her ex-colleague at BA, the first person she told of her experiences some thirty years after the war ended and who said she must record her story; Rick and Trish Longden, for getting her started on the task, and Bev Pashley for hours of early drafting and research; Lucy Ashton and Peter Butler for additional research.

I would like to thank Herti for sharing her story with me and the privilege of allowing me to gather all the strands together. Finally, we appreciate the support of all at Pen and Sword who have been instrumental in bringing this book to life.

Virginia Wells

Additional Sources

The National Archives, Kew, Richmond, Surrey; Austria Under the Nazis (online resource); Yad Vashem – The World Holocaust Remembrance Centre, Jerusalem; and the Rathaus, Friedrich-Schmidt-Platz, Wien, Vienna, Austria.